The Professional Chef's Photo-Text Series No. 1

The Professional Chef's Knife

Produced by The Learning Resources Center of
The Culinary Institute of America

FIRST EDITION

Prepared under the Guidance of Chef-Instructor Richard A. Czack of
The Culinary Institute of America

CBI

CBI Publishing Company, Inc.
51 Sleeper Street, Boston, Massachusetts 02210

THE CULINARY INSTITUTE OF AMERICA
THE LEARNING RESOURCES CENTER STAFF

Editor

MARY ELLEN GRIFFIN
Education Editor

B.A. Economics, Wellesley College; M.S., Journalism, Columbia University; Craig Claiborne Fellowship at Hotel School of Paris; Special Student, The Culinary Institute of America; Food/Wine writer.

Photographer/Graphic Designer

JOHN THOS. GRUBELL
Creative Producer - Photography/Graphics

School of Art & Design, Pratt Institute, New School of Social Research, courses at major photographic firms and studies under masters of photography. Art Director/Photographer for advertising agencies and photographic studios in New York.

Project Director

DR. SPENSER B. ROHRLICK
Director of Learning Resources Center

B.S., Central Connecticut State College; M.S., Ph.D., Instructional Technology, Syracuse University; Director, Audio Visual Center, State University of New York at New Paltz; Assistant Professor, State University of New York at Albany.

Mechanical Paste Up and Photo Retouching

KATHY SWEENEY
Graphic Artist

A.A.S., Commercial Arts, Dutchess County Community College; department store display advertising artist; commercial artist.

THE CULINARY INSTITUTE OF AMERICA
THE TECHNICAL ADVISORS

BRUNO ELLMER
Chef-Instructor

Educated in Europe. Cook in hotels in Salzburg, Villach, Badgastein and St. Wolfgang, Austria. Chef in restaurants, clubs and hotels in Montreal, Canada; New Jersey; New York; Amman, Jordan. Member 1976 U.S. Team at the International Culinary Competition.

CLAUDE GUERMONT
Chef-Instructor

Apprenticeship in Normandie, France. Commis/Cook in Paris & Cannes, France, and Menton, England; Chef de Partie, Guadaloupe; Sous Chef/Chef, restaurants in Pennsylvania.

UWE HESTNAR
Chef-Instructor

Apprenticeship in Hamburg, Germany; studies at Villanova and Cornell Universities. Cook in hotels and restaurants in Zurich, Austria; Geneva, Switzerland; Vasteras, Sweden; Isle of Wight, England; Executive Chef in hotels and restaurants in Canary Islands; Rio de Janeiro, Belim and Sao Paulo, Brazil; Pennsylvania and Washington, D.C.

ELLIOTT R. SHARRON
Chef-Instructor

A.O.S. degree, The Culinary Institute of America; studies at New York University, New Haven University. Personal Chef to Deputy Chief of Staff, U.S. Army. Sous chef and Chef at hotels, clubs, and restaurants in Connecticut, New Hampshire, New York, and Virginia.

JOSEPH W. WEISSENBERG
Chef-Instructor

A.O.S. degree, The Culinary Institute of America. Chef Steward/Executive Chef at hotels, restaurants, and clubs in Arizona, California, Connecticut, Illinois, Indiana, and Ohio; Owner/Operator Weissenberg Caterers.

JAMES J. WHITE
Chef-Instructor

Apprenticeship, U.S. Maritime Service. Chef in restaurants and a hospital in Connecticut. Chef-Instructor for State of Connecticut.

Library of Congress Cataloging in Publication Data

Culinary Institute of America. Learning Resources Center.
The professional chef's knife.

(The Professional chef's photo-text series; no. 1)
Includes index.
1. Knives. 2. Cutting. I. Czack, Richard A.
II. Title. III. Series.
TX657.K54C84   1978   641.5'89
          77-26689
ISBN 0-8436-2125-7

Printed in the United States of America

Printing (last digit): 9 8 7 6 5 4

TABLE OF CONTENTS

INTRODUCTION

The Culinary Institute of America would be remiss if it did not recognize and thank Le Roi A. Folsom, former Vice President of the Institute, who authored one of the first publications dealing expressly with this subject. The publication HOW TO MASTER THE TOOLS OF YOUR TRADE: THE FRENCH KNIFE, was published in 1965. For many years it filled an obvious void in food service education.

The Professional Chef's Knife incorporates a number of the topics treated by Le Roi Folsom's text but in a more detailed, more comprehensive and more life-like manner. The Professional Chef's Knife utilizes over two hundred photographs most of which have been shot from the chef's point of view. This photographic technique is intended to facilitate the acquisition of and subsequent transfer of knife handling skills to actual practice. Since the Institute is dedicated to providing the means to teach these skills not only to the students of The Culinary Institute of America but to the food service industry at large, the use of a photo-text such as this one is but one of the ways it seeks to provide quality education. To this end, the Institute will develop other basic photo-texts as part of its on-going educational program.

A tenet of The Culinary Institute of America is that in order to become a skilled professional chef, mastery of the basic skills must come first. The Chef's Knife is one of the chef's most important professional tools. Few other implements can perform so many tasks in a skilled hand, or last a lifetime (and then some) given proper care and respect.

The Chef's Knife, properly chosen and handled, is not a complicated utensil. In order to make the most of it, one must understand its construction and use. One must also recognize, respect, and care for the finely honed edge.

The Institute has endeavored to present a comprehensive view of the various types of Chef's Knives readily available on the market, and of the several accepted methods of handling them.

When purchasing a Chef's Knife, consider the pro's and con's of the various types, and choose one that is right for your hand. Study the sections in this text on care and handling, and practice, practice, practice!

The Chef's Knife, like all our other cutting tools, is a descendent of utensils used a million years ago. While the bone, piece of wood, or primative stone hatchet of pre-historic times may not seem to have much in common with glistening stainless steel, they have in common two factors - a sharp edge on a hard substance.

Therefore, one of the most important aspects to consider in choosing a Chef's Knife is the material of which the blade is made. This is the most functional part of the tool, and the one which will cause the most problems if not of the right quality.

Man's discovery of iron and its use (about 4,000 years ago) was one of the first breakthroughs in the development of the knives we use today. This element, one of the most common, could be melted and shaped into tools. The first iron knives took to sharpening far better than any of their predecessors. They had two big disadvantages - being chronically rusty and being either too soft from slow cooling or hard enough, but brittle, if cooled quickly.

Steel is a mixture of at least 80% iron and up to 20% other elements. Carbon steel, the first kind known to man, was made about 3,000 years ago. This alloy of carbon and iron is the most similar to pure cast iron and is still a popular material for Chef's Knives.

Other types of steel have been developed over the years, and those which are most important in the manufacture of knife blades are stainless (with a minimum of 4% chromium and/or nickel) and high carbon stainless. The latter is considered by many authorities to be the best, as it has the advantages of high carbon stainless and stainless steels but the disadvantages of neither.

We also hear of certain Super-Stainless Alloys for knives whose manufacturers promise that no sharpening will ever be needed. Beware, this really means that the steel is so hard that it can never be sharpened.

The Rockwell Scale is an indicator of the hardness of particular materials, the higher the number, the harder the material. Most Chef's Knives fall into the range of 54-57 on the Rockwell Scale, most sharpening steels between 64 and 67.

Sharpening is most efficiently accomplished through the abrasive action of a material harder (higher on the Rockwell Scale) than the item to be sharpened.

Sharpening will be discussed further in the sections on Sharpening Steels and Sharpening Stones.

METAL	ADVANTAGES	DISADVANTAGES
Carbon Steel	Takes and holds an excellent edge	Corrodes extremely easily, even while in use (for example, on garlic or onions) Not practical for use in humid (especially salt air) climates Not practical for use with high acid foods (such as citrus fruits) Brittle
Stainless Steel	Resistant to abrasion Resistant to corrosion Great tensile strength	Difficult to sharpen, does not take edge easily Difficult to maintain edge
High Carbon Stainless Steel	Takes edge better than stainless steel May be used in any climate and on any foods Will not pit or rust	Special care must be taken to use proper (hard enough) sharpening steel
Super-Stainless Alloy Steel	Looks pretty	So hard that it is virtually impossible to sharpen NOT RECOMMENDED

BLADE SIZES

The primary factor in considering which size blade to use is your comfort in handling the knife; the comments below are suggestions which might be helpful in choosing a Chef's Knife to purchase or to accomplish a particular kitchen task.

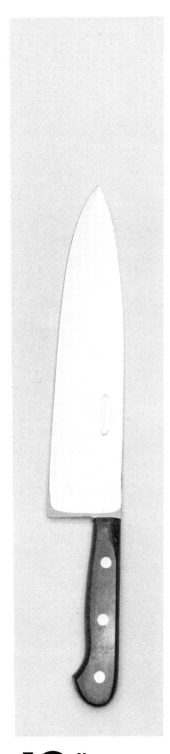

14" 35.6cm

This long blade can make bulk work (such as chopping large amounts of parsley) more efficient and easier. It is also effective for slicing large pieces of cooked meat (although other types of knives are better suited to this task).

12" 30.5cm

Very similar in appearance and feel (although the 10 inch is the more popular), these two sizes may be considered all-purpose knives. Either of these, the most common sizes of Chef's Knives, may be used for any dicing, chopping, mincing, etc.

10" 25.4cm

8" 20.3cm

The 8 inch blade provides a maximum of comfort and control. It is the best *first* Chef's Knife to own, particularly for people with small hands. It is especially handy for doing detailed work, such as mincing shallots and fileting certain types of fish, particularly if the blade is somewhat flexible.

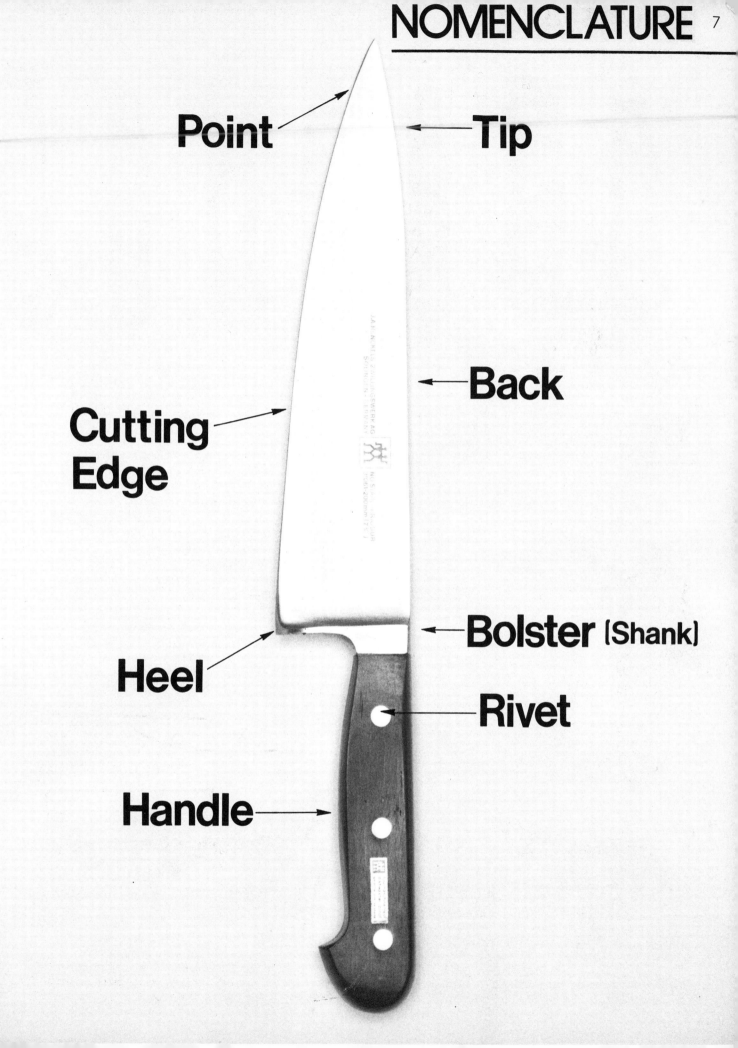

Point

Tip

Back

Cutting Edge

Bolster (Shank)

Heel

Rivet

Handle

KNIFE HANDLE

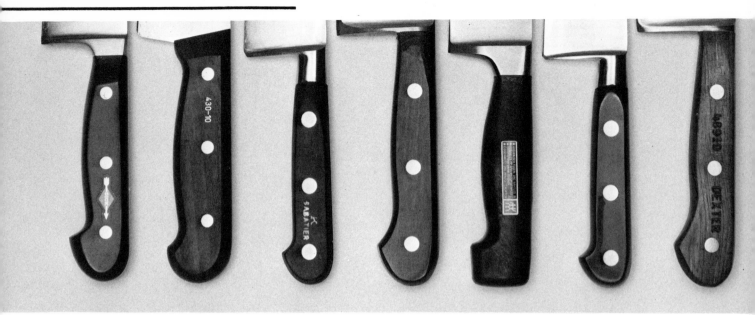

The correct handle is almost as important as the blade in the Chef's Knife. When shopping for this tool, a large part of the purchasing decision rests in actually picking up a number of knives to see how well they each balance in your hand (as is discussed on the facing page). There are other important considerations as well:

A. *Shape of the Handle* - Generally, the simpler the shape, the most likely the handle is to be comfortable to work with.

B. *Material of the Handle* - The most highly regarded material is Brazilian rosewood, because of its natural non-slip grain, hardness and attractive appearance.

Many other woods are also acceptable, as are many plastic impregnated woods or plastics. Whenever dealing with a plastic-type handle, be careful to avoid anything too enthusiastically laminated or otherwise 'protected,' for the coating may be extremely slippery.

Plastic-type knives are the most sanitary, although some may have a tendency to crack after a few years use. (Wood, if not properly cared for can do the same thing.) Hard rubber and plastic handles which completely envelop the tang are also made. The more common Chef's Knives' handles, made of plastic or plastic impregnated wood, allow the tang to be visible (and thus indicate top quality).

C. *The Tang* - This is the section of the blade which extends through the handle. The finer the knife, the fuller a tang it will have. This increases the stability of the knife, makes it longer lasting, and helps lend weight and balance to the handle.

The joining of the handle and the tang should be almost perfectly smooth. Gaps create an abrasive area which can irritate the hand and are unsanitary harboring places for microorganisms. The juncture of the handle and the rivets should also be smooth.

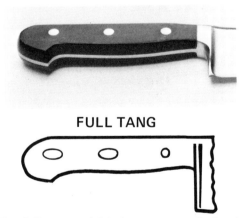

FULL TANG

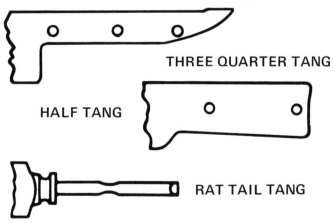

THREE QUARTER TANG

HALF TANG

RAT TAIL TANG

The full tang, which is recommended as best, is secured by three rivets and is visible on all sides of the handle. The three quarter tang also has three rivets, but the metal is completely encased in the handle material on the lower edge.

The half tang, with two rivets, is equally visible on the upper and lower edges, but extends only a fraction of the way through the handle. The rat tail tang is completely encased in the handle material.

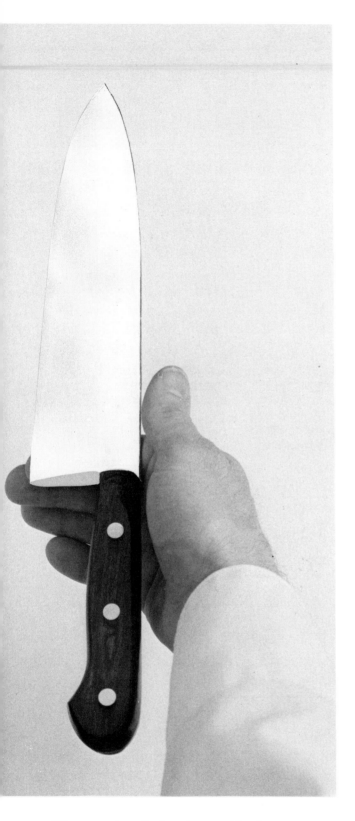

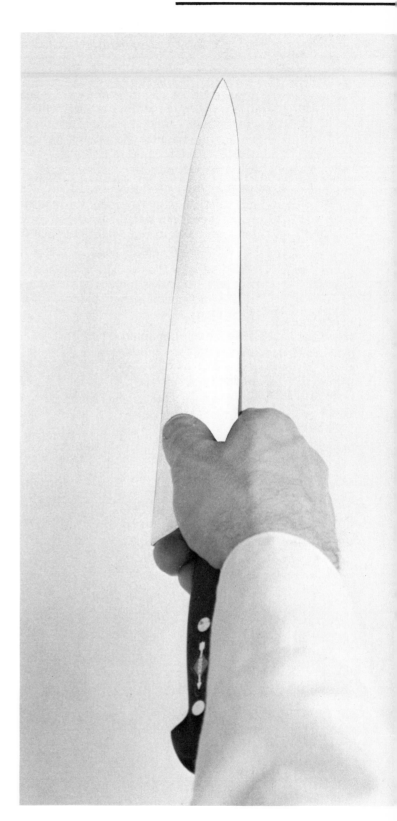

There are two factors to consider in determining the balance of a Chef's Knife - the knife itself and your hand.

The knife should feel secure and in control when resting horizontally on your open hand (as in the picture on the left). The heavier the handle, the farther back you will want to hold it, and the more control you will have. Knives with a full tang can be expected to be heavier in the handle area.

When you actually grip the knife (utilizing one of the three methods illustrated on pages 34 - 39), it should feel comfortable and you should not have to exert pressure to keep it horizontal.

In order to make the best choice when purchasing a Chef's Knife, test each one you are considering for proper balance. Sometimes even knives of the same manufacturer and model will feel different in your hand.

A quality Chef's Knife is not an inexpensive tool, and thus deserves proper care, which will lengthen its life, make it a safer object with which to work, and minimize the amount of times you have to sharpen it.

A few basic rules:

NEVER soak a knife - this is bad for the blade and most handles (especially those made of wood, which can warp), and is extremely dangerous as someone might put their hands in the water and be cut.

NEVER put a knife in a dishwasher; the intense heat will distort the molecular structure of the blade. It might also be damaged if it hits other items.

NEVER be careless about where the knife is put down; if it can bump into other items (even the side of a drawer), the blade may be damaged.

NEVER use the cutting edge to scrape food off of a cutting board.

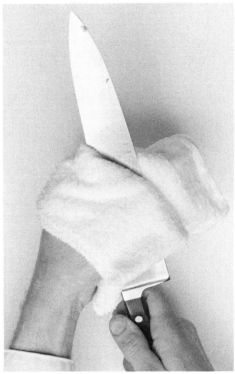

1 Wipe the blade by hand with a damp cloth after each use, taking care to wipe from the back edge of the blade, not the cutting edge, and wiping away from you. Sudsy water may be employed. Dry immediately.

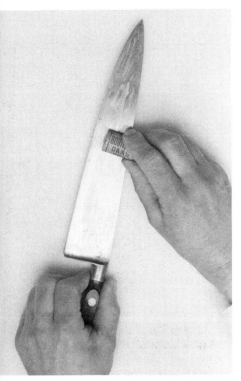

2 Spots may be removed from any knife by rubbing briskly with powdered cleanser and a wet cork (although the method is needed and used primarily on carbon steel). This will leave an attractive sheen on the blade.

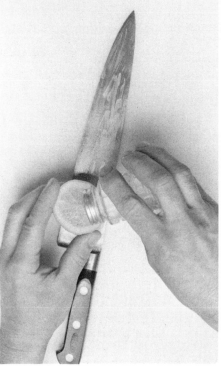

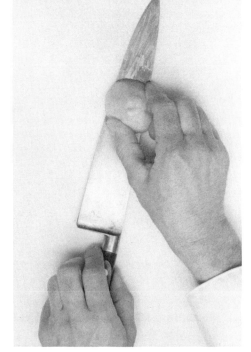

3 Another effective method for cleaning the blade is to sprinkle salt on a half lemon and then rub the blade. This will help rid the blade of stains. Be sure to stay away from the cutting edge and to wipe the blade after performing this procedure. The knife may be sanitized by washing with soap and water, and rinsing in hot tap water.

There are four things to consider in storing your Chef's Knife: Safety, Protection of the Blade, Cleanliness, and Convenience. The following are some of the many approved ways of storing knives.

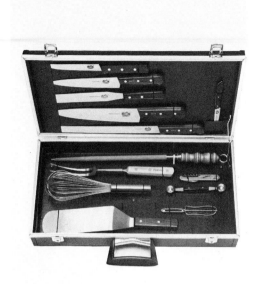

Designed for the professional chef, this portable box is a safe, convenient home for a large collection of kitchen utensils. A protective sheath for each and every one of the knives in the box is a must; many professional chefs utilize a tool box or other metal box for this purpose.

This type of wooden holder is mounted firmly on the wall, never on the side of a table, as the exposed blade can present a safety hazard to workers or passers-by. It should be high enough to be out of reach of children but low enough to be within reach of adults using or putting away the knives. The blade must be wiped before being placed in the holder to avoid the accumulation of dirt.

The tip of a knife which must be stored in a drawer (which contains only knives and which is opened and closed very gently) may be protected with a cork. Cutting one side of the cork so that it rests flat will stabilize the knife and minimize movement. If the knife is to be stored for a long time, a light coating of petroleum jelly will help protect the blade. It must be removed completely before the knife is used again.

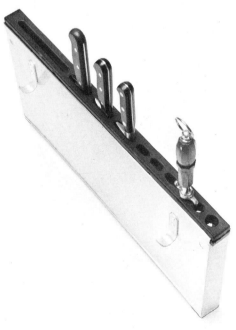

Similar to the wooden holder above, this steel and rubber is more sanitary. The steel is not porous like wood and cannot harbour microorganisms; the rubber is removable and may be washed and sanitized (even in the dishwasher).

This wooden block with slots for knives provides excellent protection for knives, and does not leave edges exposed. This type of holder comes in a variety of sizes and shapes. Blades must be carefully cleaned before being put into the slots, which are extremely difficult to clean.

Most magnetic holders are not recommended because of the danger of slippage of knives. This model magnetic holder does, however, have a protective holder at the bottom which provides some protection. Do not attempt to store particularly heavy knives on a magnetic holder.

SAFETY

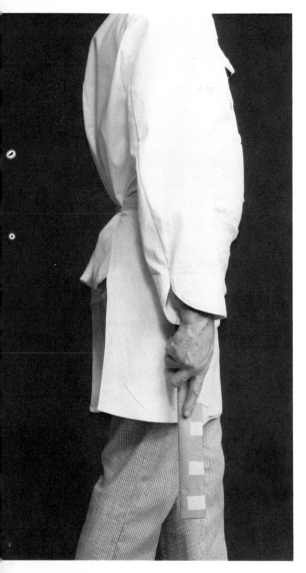

Never carry your Chef's Knife unprotected. Before moving from the work table, put the protective sheath on the knife; carry it at your side, the tip pointing toward the floor. Hold the knife firmly with your index finger securing the sheath. Put the knife in a safe place as soon as you reach your destination.

The most important aspect of owning a Chef's Knife is understanding some basic, common sense safety concepts. Your knife is extremely sharp, and deserves respect, but not fear, and understanding, but not over-confidence.

DO keep a sharp edge. The sharper the edge on your Chef's Knife, the easier it is to work with. A dull edge means that you have less control and have to use more pressure, both of which are good ways to get cut. Also, this inaccurate cutting can damage the food with which you are working.

DON'T run your fingers down the edge to check the sharpness.

DON'T attempt to catch a falling knife; *let it fall* and get your feet out of the way.

DO wear leather footwear for protection, in case a knife falls on your foot.

DON'T ever put a knife in dish water to soak. Besides being bad for the blade, this presents a safety hazard to whoever puts their hands into the water.

DON'T put the knife in the dishwasher.

DON'T hide a knife under anything.

DO use the right knife for the right job.

DO employ safe storage techniques.

DO cut away from your body and away from your hands.

DON'T use a Chef's Knife as a bottle opener or any other tool it is not.

DON'T place vegetables or fruit that you are cutting in your palm.

DON'T let the knife hang over the edge of the table.

DON'T use a Chef's Knife if you are drowsy or not feeling well. Any lack of attention or control multiplies your chances of being injured.

DON'T attempt to hand the Chef's Knife to someone else. Put it down on the table and let them pick it up.

DO keep your eyes on your work.

DON'T carry your knife away from the work area. If you must move from one area to another with a Chef's Knife in your hand, follow the adjacent instructions.

The photographs on this page originally appeared in *Popular Science* magazine (February, 1977). They are of interest to any owner of a Chef's Knife, as they illustrate what its edge looks like under a microscope. Note the saw-like ridges, formed through proper sharpening in *one direction*.

1 *Oil Honed Edge, 3000x* - This edge was honed on a sharpening stone lubricated in the traditional fashion with oil. Note the gouges, which John A. Juranitch, author of the *Popular Science* article, attributes to pieces of steel in suspension in the oil. (Many chefs, however, feel that a stone without oil or water can damage a knife.)

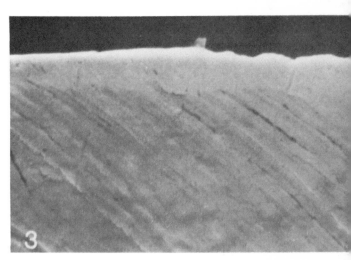

2 *Dry Honed Edge, 3000x* - This edge was honed without the use of oil or water. Note that the appearance is somewhat smoother than in picture Number 1. Also note the toothlike appearance of both edges, caused by the texture of the sharpening stone.

3 *Dry Honed Edge, Properly Steeled, 3000x* - Note how the action of the steel has smoothed the edge to eliminate the saw-like ridges, maximizing sharpness.

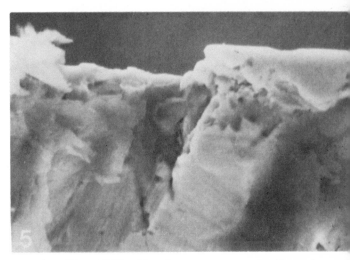

4 *Worn Edge, 1000x* - A sharp edge was run several times over wood, with the resulting damage to the edge, which now requires a repeat honing on the stone. The same damage can result from improper care and handling of the knife, such as throwing it in a drawer. Correct handling will protect your knife from this kind of damage.

5 *Worn Edge, 7000x* - Note how craters are actually made in the edge when the knife becomes worn. This is, of course, repairable through a new honing.

A sharpening stone is a worthwhile investment to make when you obtain a Chef's Knife. It is possible to avoid the use of a sharpening stone by bringing your knife to a reputable professional sharpener every time it becomes dull, but the convenience and economy of learning to sharpen your own knife is a real plus, especially if you take your cutting seriously and want to ensure yourself of having a fine edge all the time.

There are a number of kinds and sizes of sharpening stones, several of which are depicted on the left. Carborundum stone is the most common material used in making sharpening stones, but you'll also find products made of abrasives such as sandstone, silicon carbide, silicon dioxide, aluminum oxide and others. Shop for a sharpening stone from a reliable dealer and ask him/her to recommend a material if you are in doubt.

The size of the sharpening stone is a matter of personal preference although the standard size is 8 inches x 2 inches x 13/16 inches. The advantage of a larger stone is its greater surface area which makes it best to work with; the disadvantage is its bulkiness. A smaller stone is handier to carry and store, but is not as easy to work with. A simple, flat shape is generally the most functional. The miniature ceramic steel on page 21 is so hard that it can be considered a true sharpening stone, although it is in the shape of a steel.

Sharpening stones are available in three textures:

A. *Coarse* - Very rough, for use when the knife is in extremely poor condition. Hopefully, your knife will not get so badly gouged as to require sharpening on this type stone.

B. *Medium* - The all purpose, most frequently used texture. In sharpening a Chef's Knife, this may be the only stone you will need.

C. *Fine* - A very fine texture which will hone the knife to razor sharpness. This may be too sharp for the Chef's Knife, although very useful for boning knives or other finer tools.

1 Two sharpening stones are shown here, both of them dual purpose stones, comprised of a medium and a fine hone sandwiched together. Single purpose stones are also generally found in this shape.

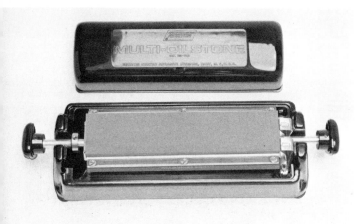

2 This tool has three stones (coarse, medium and fine) on a turntable which operates like a ferris wheel, revolving easily and including a mechanism to lock it in place. There is an oil reserve at the bottom in which the two stones not in use rest. The construction allows for stones to be removed and replaced as they wear out.

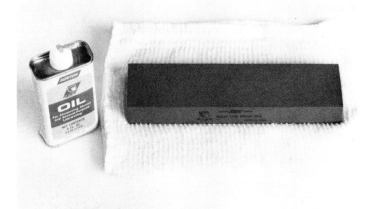

3 When preparing to use the sharpening stone, first place it on a damp towel or piece of rubber netting to prevent slippage. (A wooden or rubber fitting around the stone can also serve this purpose.) Some professional chefs use mineral oil or water (never vegetable oil) to lubricate the stone and increase its efficiency. Others feel that this actually decreases its value because steel filings in the slick may make gouges in the knife, and oil helps these particles become embedded in the stone. The latter will not happen with water lubrication. It is possible to remove the oil from a sharpening stone by boiling it with water and chlorine bleach (or vinegar) and baking it to dry out.

The objective in using the sharpening stone is to wear away the blade to a two edged point. There are many very effective ways of sharpening the Chef's Knife, and whether you use one of the methods shown or another, the important rules to follow are:

A. Hold the knife at a *constant 20° angle* to the stone.

B. *Always sharpen in the same direction*, to create sawlike ridges in the knife's edge.

C. Make the strokes on each side in *equal number and of equal pressure.*

D. If the knife is particularly dull, start with a coarse stone, and then use a medium stone. Normally, you should use only the medium stone in sharpening the Chef's Knife. (Utilize a fine stone if a razor sharp edge is required.)

E. As a general rule, make five (5) strokes on each side of the blade, for a total of ten (10). Stop in any case when a burr begins to form.

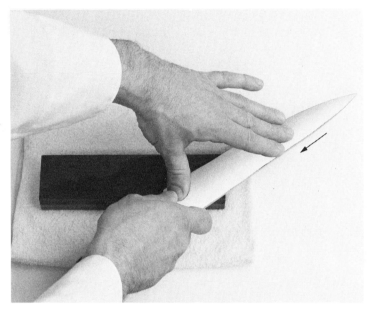

1 Grasp the knife firmly. Use the four most comfortable fingers of the guiding hand (the one not holding the knife) to stabilize it and maintain constant pressure. Set the knife at a 20° angle, touching the stone as in the photograph.

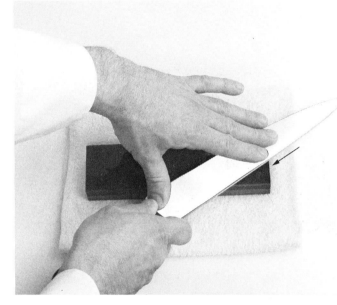

2 Begin to draw the knife across the stone, gently, but with abrasive action on the blade.

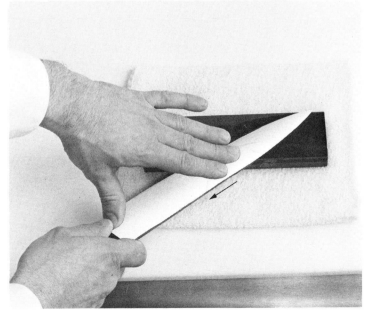

3 Continue the movement in a smooth action.

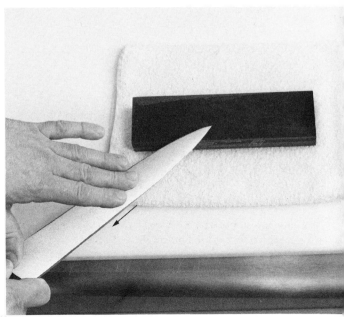

4 Draw the knife off of the stone in a smooth fashion, providing the same abrasion for the tip of the blade as you did for the other parts.

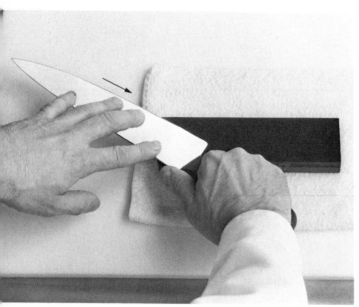

5 Turn the knife around so that the side of the blade just sharpened is now facing up. Use the guiding hand to stabilize it and maintain constant pressure. Set the knife at the same angle as used for the first side and position the knife as in the picture.

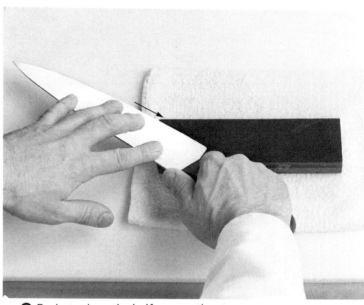

6 Begin to draw the knife across the stone.

7 Continue the movement smoothly.

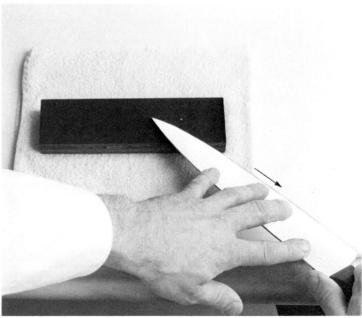

8 Draw the knife off of the stone in a smooth fashion, providing the same abrasion for the tip as you did for the other areas.

The objective in using the sharpening stone is to wear away the blade to a two edged point. There are many very effective ways of sharpening the Chef's Knife, and whether you use one of the methods shown or another, the important rules to follow are:

A. Hold the knife at a *constant 20° angle* to the stone.
B. *Always sharpen in the same direction,* to create sawlike ridges in the knife's edge.
C. Make the strokes on each side in *equal number and of equal pressure.*
D. If the knife is particularly dull, start with a coarse stone, and then use a medium stone. Normally, you should use only the medium stone in sharpening the Chef's Knife. (Utilize a fine stone if a razor sharp edge is required.)
E. As a general rule, make five (5) strokes on each side of the blade, for a total of ten (10). Stop in any case when a burr begins to form.

KNIFE
20°
SHARPENING STONE

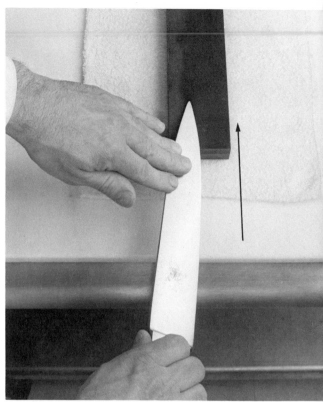

1 Grasp the knife firmly. Use the guiding hand to stabilize it and maintain constant pressure. Set the knife at a 20° angle. Position the knife touching the stone as in the picture, and begin to draw the knife over the surface of the stone.

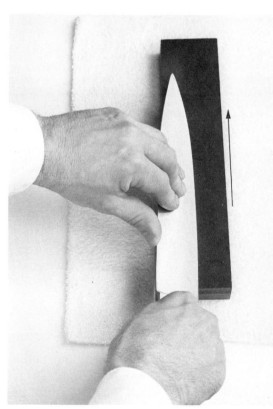

2 Continue the movement in a smooth motion.

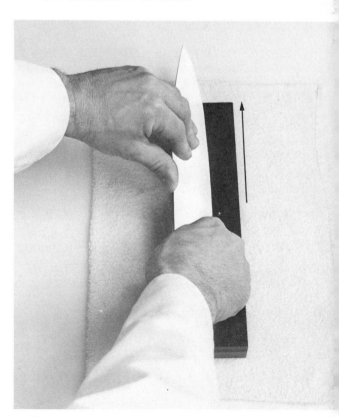

3 Draw the knife off of the stone in a smooth fashion, not neglecting to pass the last few inches of the blade over the stone.

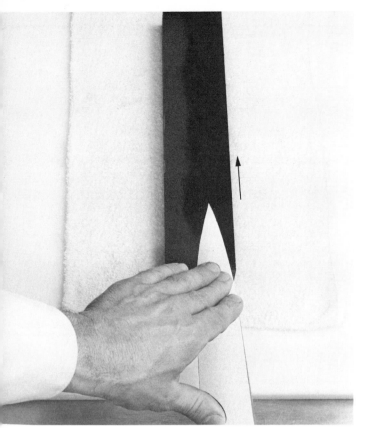

4 Turn the knife around so that the side of the blade just sharpened is now facing up. Use the guiding hand (the hand not holding the knife) to stabilize it and maintain constant pressure. Set the knife at the same angle as used for the first side and position the knife as in the picture.

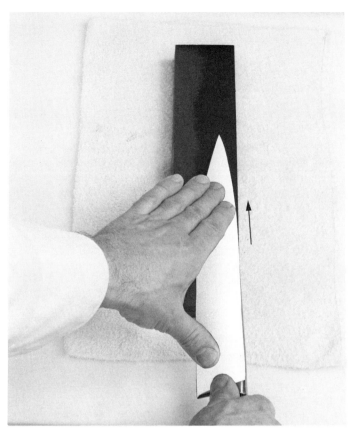

5 Begin to draw the knife across the stone.

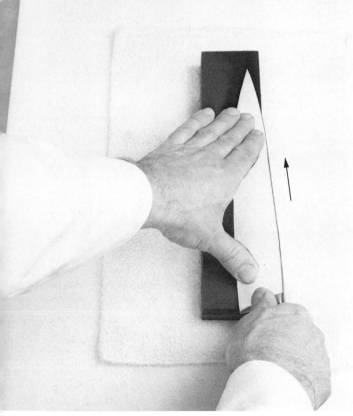

6 Continue the movement in a smooth motion.

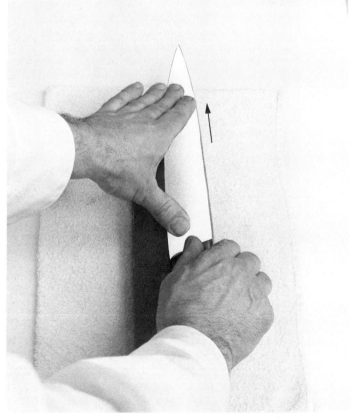

7 Draw the knife off of the stone in a smooth fashion, not neglecting to pass the last few inches of the blade over the stone.

The sharpening steel is an even more important adjunct to the Chef's Knife than is the sharpening stone, as it is a tool that should be used very frequently to help maintain the edge, and always used after honing on the stone.

To clean a sharpening steel, wipe with a cloth which has been dampened with vinegar.

The role of the sharpening steel is three-fold:

A. *To true the edge* - The teeth left by the action of the sharpening stone aid in cutting, but it is advantageous to rub the very edge of the blade to perfect smoothness. Also, the edge may bend somewhat in normal usage. The steel, if properly used, will perfect the edge. (See Picture No. 3 on page 13.)

B. *To realign the molecules of the blade* - In the manufacturing of fine Chef's Knives, a great deal of attention is given to the development of properly aligned metal molecules. Through a normal use, these may come awry. Some sharpening steels (the metallic ones) are magnetized and will serve to correct this problem, particularly important in carbon steel blades. Also, metal particles will cling to a magnetized steel, which prevents their getting into food.

C. *To actually sharpen the blade* - In some cases, e.g., when using certain ceramic sharpening steels, the sharpening steel will actually perform this function.

When choosing a steel consider these factors:

A. *The Shaft* - The material of which the shaft is made must be harder than the metal it is to sharpen. Make sure that when you purchase a steel it is from a reputable dealer, and that you specify the type and length of blade which is to be used with it. Steels may be made of steel, as well as of various ceramics.

Also, consider the texture of the shaft. Some are coarser than others, and the type of grain you choose should be a function of the kind of sharpening you intend to do. Some steels are made with two different grains on either side of the shaft.

B. *The Handle and Guard* - The handle should be of a material which will last and which will not be slippery if wet. One extremely important aspect of the steel is the guard, a protrusion of metal which is placed between the handle and the shaft for the protection of your hand while steeling. Try to purchase a steel with an adequate guard. If you cannot avoid using a steel without one, always use Steeling Methods No. 2 or No. 3, both of which involve aiming the knife away from you.

C. *The Construction* - As in any purchase, you will want your steel to be sturdy and to have the promise of many years' service. If you possess a knife rack or holder, you might want to invest in a cylindrical (round) steel. Don't sacrifice usefulness for fashion if a flatter model (which actually has more sharpening area) would be more functional for your needs.

NOMENCLATURE

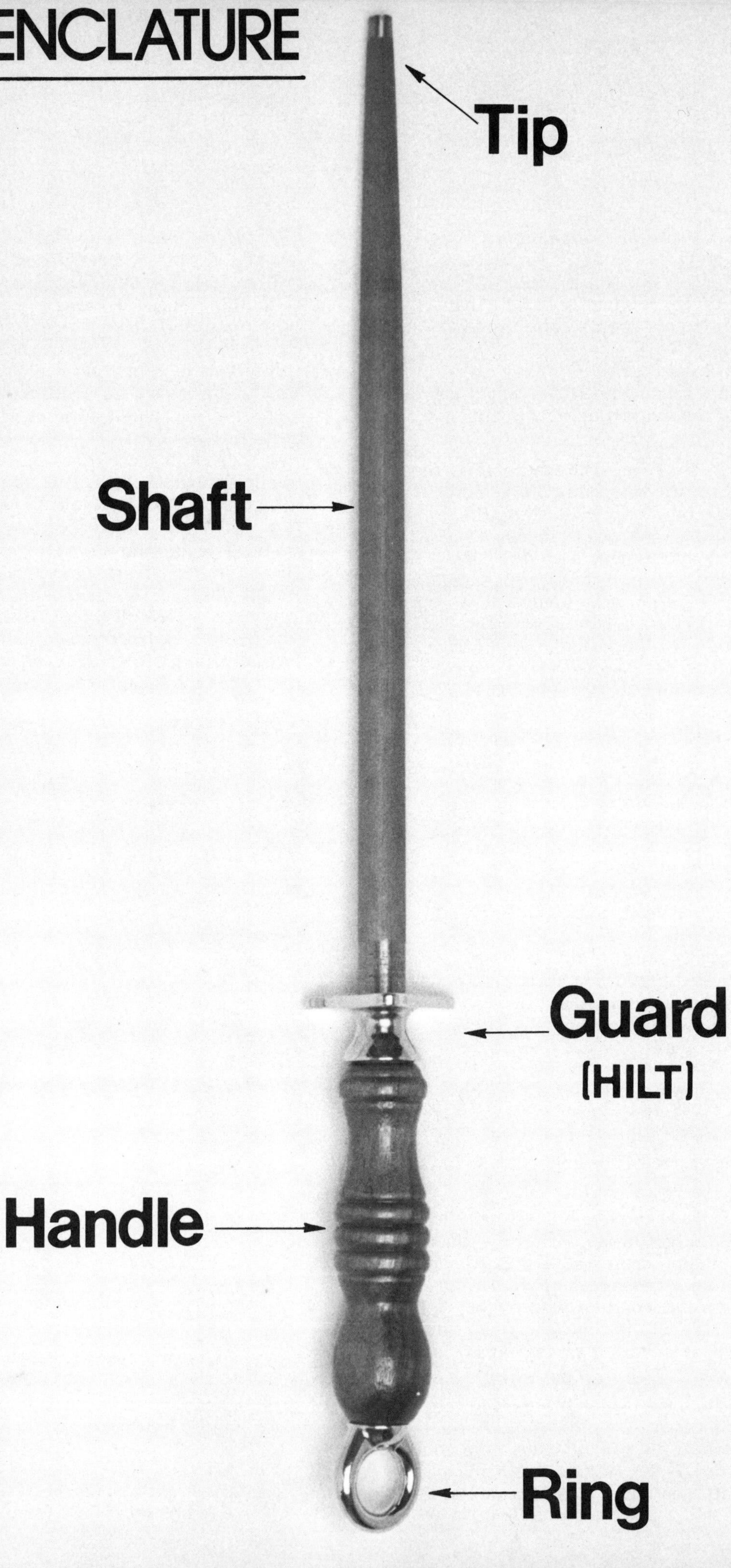

Tip

Shaft

Guard
(HILT)

Handle

Ring

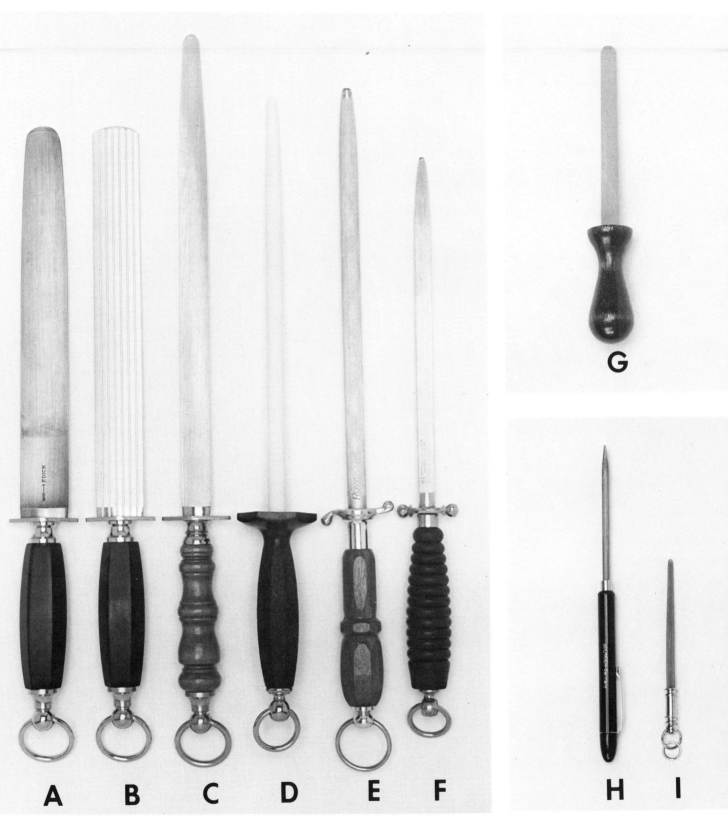

This small sampling illustrates some of the many kinds of high quality sharpening steels available: **A.** Flat; fine grain; magnetized; 11 inch (27.9 cm) steel shaft. **B.** Flat; fine and coarse grains alternating in the barlike structure; magnetized; 11 inch (27.9 cm) steel shaft. **C.** Oval, elongated; fine grain; magnetized; 13 1/3 inch (33.9 cm) steel shaft. **D.** Cylindrical; smooth; 12 inch (30.5 cm) ceramic shaft. **E.** Cylindrical, fine grain; magnetized; 12 inch (30.5 cm) steel shaft. **F.** Cylindrical; fine grain; magnetized; 10 inch (25.4 cm) steel shaft. **G.** Cylindrical; abrasive but smooth; 3 1/2 inch (8.9 cm) ceramic shaft; may serve same sharpening function as the sharpening stone. **H.** Cylindrical; fine grain; 3 inch (7.6 cm) steel shaft; looks like a pen when shaft is reversed and secured inside casing. **I.** Cylindrical; fine grain; magnetized; 2 3/4 inch (7.0 cm) steel shaft.

HANDLES AND GUARDS

While the shaft is clearly the most functional part of the sharpening steel, its other components merit attention as well. The Guard is the most important safety feature of this tool and should thus be taken very seriously. The Handle and Ring are also areas which will influence your comfort and convenience when using the sharpening steel.

The Guard - This protrusion is extremely important because of its function in protecting the user of the steel from injury, as many popular strokes in using this tool require that the knife be directed toward the body. Most guards provide protection on two sides of the steel (some on three) and the user of these types should be careful to use protected areas only. It is recommended to avoid guardless steels, unless there is a compelling reason not to. Even if you personally avoid using the strokes which would be dangerous on this type steel, you have no assurance that someone else less knowledgeable than yourself is not going to pick up the steel, use strokes they are accustomed to, forget about the absence of the guard, and injure themselves.

The Handle - Like the handle of the Chef's Knife itself, this should be comfortable in your hand and of functional design. Handles are commonly made of wood, ebonite, plastic or hard rubber. They are often designed with an eye toward style (which does not necessarily diminish their usefulness).

The Ring - The reason for the ring is completely functional, to enable the sharpening steel to be hung on a wall hook or on a special clasp on a butcher's apron. It is also a contributing factor to the attractiveness of this tool.

There are several important guidelines in making the most effective use of the sharpening steel:

A.   Use a featherlike stroke rather than a grinding action and work at a 20° angle. Make strokes evenly and consistantly.

B.   Listen for a melodic ring as you use the steel; if you hear a grinding noise, you are applying too much pressure.

C.   Use only five (5) strokes on each side of the blade. Over steeling will distort the edge. Should these 10 strokes be inadequate, you should use the sharpening stone (which should have been used in the first place).

D.   Do not hit the blade against the guard.

E.   Hold the steel with the thumb safely tucked behind the guard.

1 Start with the knife in a vertical position, lightly touching the steel and at a 20° angle to it. The steel should be one arm's length away from the body.

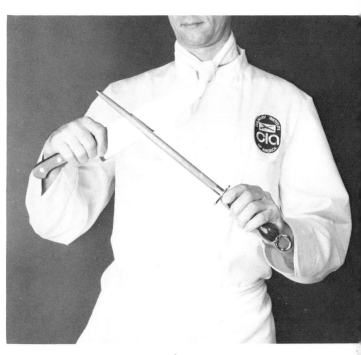

2 Begin to pass the knife along the length of the steel, maintaining light pressure and a constant 20° angle. Note the wrist action and how the arms stay virtually still.

3 Continue in a smooth motion. Note how the entire length of the steel is being used.

4 Complete the movement by passing the tip of the knife across the steel. Note the importance of the guard, and that the steel is being held so that the protrusions of metal will protect the hand.

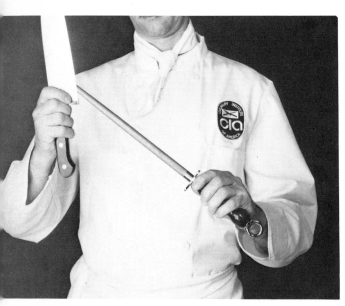

5 Again hold the knife in a vertical position, with the opposite side of the blade touching the opposite side of the steel in order to perform the same actions on the reverse side of the knife. The knife should be at a 20° angle to the steel.

6 Begin to pass the knife along the length of the steel, maintaining light pressure and a constant 20° angle. Again note the action of the wrist.

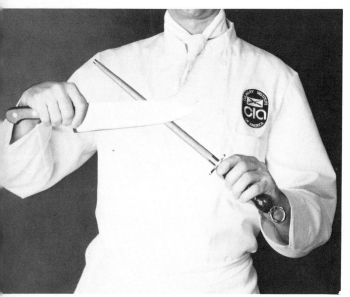

7 Continue in a smooth motion. Note how the entire length of the steel is being used.

8 Complete the movement by passing the tip of the knife across the steel. Again, note the importance of the guard.

There are several important guidelines in making the most effective use of the sharpening steel:

A. Use a featherlike stroke rather than a grinding action and work at a 20° angle. Make strokes evenly and consistantly.

B. Listen for a melodic ring as you use the steel; if you hear a grinding noise, you are applying too much pressure.

C. Use only five (5) strokes on each side of the blade. Over steeling will distort the edge. Should these 10 strokes be inadequate, you should use the sharpening stone (which should have been used in the first place).

D. Beware of people or things around or in front of you as you steel away from your body.

1 Start with the knife and steel crossed at an arm's length in front of you, lightly touching at a 20° angle to each other at the point of contact. Start at the guard, the heel of the knife touching the part of the steel closest to you. Finish with the knife and steel tip to tip.

2 Begin to pass the knife along the length of the steel, maintaining light pressure and a constant 20° angle. Note that the steel is being held perfectly still, and only the wrist and arm of the hand holding the knife are moving.

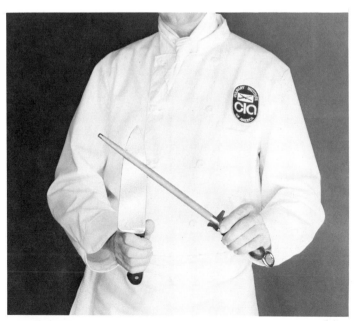

3 Continue in a smooth motion. Note how the entire length of the steel is being used.

4 Complete the movement by passing the tip of the knife across the tip of the steel.

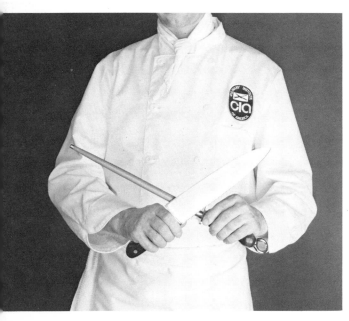

5 Now cross the opposite sides of the knife and steel in front of you, lightly touching and at a 20° angle to each other at the point of contact.

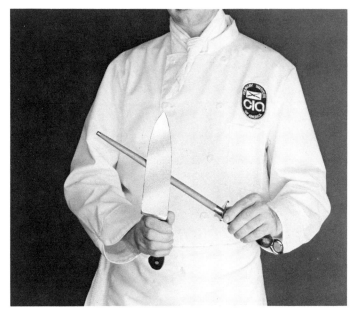

6 Begin to pass the knife along the length of the steel, maintaining light pressure and a constant 20° angle. The motion is away from the body.

7 Continue in a smooth motion. Note how the entire length of the steel is being used.

8 Complete the movement by passing the tip of the knife across the steel.

There are several important guidelines in making the most effective use of the sharpening steel:

A. Use a featherlike stroke rather than a grinding action and work at a 20° angle. Make strokes evenly and consistantly.

B. Listen for a melodic ring as you use the steel; if you hear a grinding noise, you are applying too much pressure.

C. Use only five (5) strokes on each side of the blade. Over steeling will distort the edge. Should these 10 strokes be inadequate, you should use the sharpening stone (which should have been used in the first place).

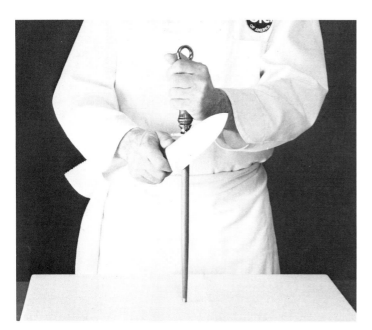

1 Hold the steel in a near vertical position with the tip resting on the cutting board (set on a wet towel if it is slippery) or on some other non-slippery surface. Place the knife pointing slightly up-ward so that it lightly touches the steel and rests at a 20° angle to it. Start at the guard, the heel of the knife touching the part of the steel closest to you. Finish with the knife and steel tip to tip.

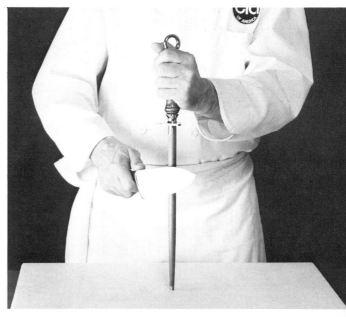

2 Begin to pass the knife along the length of the steel, maintaining light pressure and a constant 20° angle. Note that this is an arm action, not a wrist action.

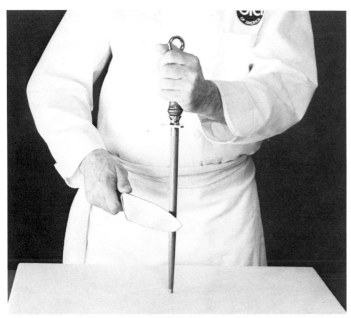

3 Continue in a smooth motion. Note how the entire length of the steel is being used.

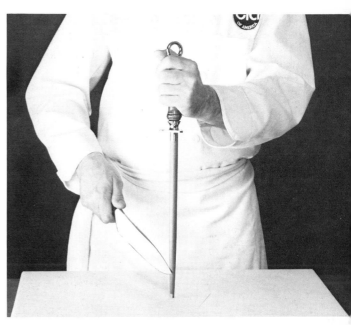

4 Complete the movement by passing the tip of the knife across the steel.

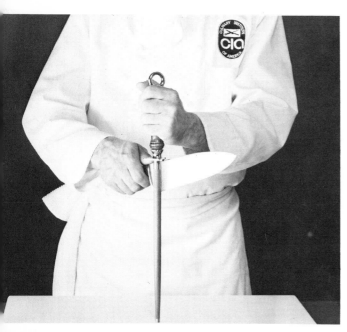

5 Again place the knife in contact with the steel, using the opposite sides of those used before. The knife should be at a 20° angle to the steel.

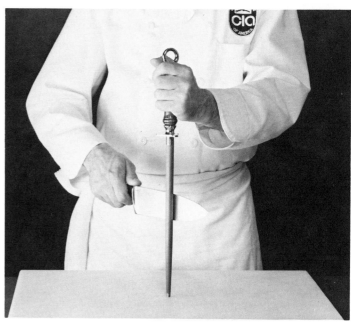

6 Begin to pass the knife along the length of the steel, maintaining light pressure and a constant 20° angle. Note that this is an arm action, not a wrist action.

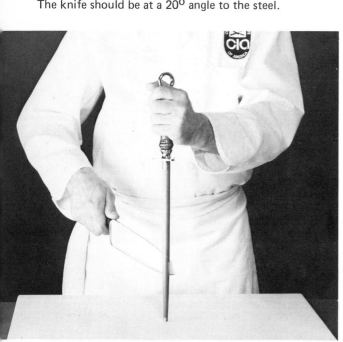

7 Continue in a smooth motion. Note how the entire length of the steel is being used.

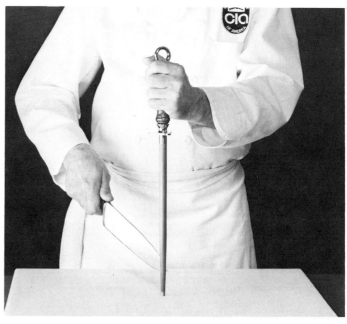

8 Complete the movement by passing the tip of the knife across the steel.

There are several important guidelines in making the most effective use of the sharpening steel:

A. Use a featherlike stroke rather than a grinding action and work at a 20° angle. Make strokes evenly and consistantly.

B. Listen for a melodic ring as you use the steel; if you hear a grinding noise, you are applying too much pressure.

C. Use only five (5) strokes on each side of the blade. Over steeling will distort the edge. Should these 10 strokes be inadequate, you should use the sharpening stone (which should have been used in the first place).

D. Do not hit the blade against the guard.

E. Hold the steel with the thumb safely tucked behind the guard.

1 Start with the knife in a vertical position, lightly touching the steel and with the blade at a 20° angle to it. The steel should be horizontal, and held one arm's length away from the body.

2 Begin to pass the knife along the length of the steel, maintaining light pressure and a constant 20° angle. Note the wrist action and how the arms stay virtually still.

3 Continue in a smooth motion. Note how the entire length of the steel is being used.

4 Complete the movement by passing the tip of the knife across the steel. Note the importance of the guard, and that the steel is being held so that the protrusions of metal will protect the hand.

5 Again place the knife in contact with the steel, only with the opposite sides touching.

6 Begin to pass the knife along the length of the steel, maintaining light pressure and a 20° angle. Note that this is a wrist action.

7 Continue in a smooth motion. Note how the entire length of the steel is being used.

8 Complete the movement by passing the tip of the knife across the steel.

There are three major factors to consider in choosing a cutting surface: cleanliness and cleanability, resilience and gentleness to the knife's edge.

The importance of the concept of keeping the cutting surface clean is obvious, as it comes into contact with food which people are ultimately going to eat. The most sanitary materials for cutting boards are hard rubber and plastic, which are, in fact, the only materials which some states will permit professional establishments to purchase.

Wooden cutting boards can also be extremely sanitary. However, they require appropriate care - scraping clean and sanding away ruts and nicks which can collect debris and germs.

Resilience is important to the professional chef's comfort in working. A board which is not resilient (for example, made of a ceramic material) will make the cutting job much harder on the arm holding the knife, make the person much less effective and less comfortable, and consequently, make the operation less safe.

Never use your Chef's Knife on a metal or other hard surface which will distort the blade and shorten the life of this fine tool. The Chef's Knife deserves this respect and indeed requires it if it is to have a long, productive life.

This plastic cutting board meets all the criteria for cleanliness, but has the disadvantages of little or no resilience, a tendency toward developing ruts and chips (which might find their way into food) and a dulling action on the knife blade.

The hard rubber of which this rimmed board is made is sanitary and resilient. It is especially handy when being used for cutting wet or juicy items, as liquids released from the foods are trapped and prevented from running elsewhere. Some chefs find that the texture of a rubber surface slows them down when working quickly. Also, the rim can interfere with cutting at the edge.

The wooden cutting board is still most professional chefs' favorite, in spite of the extra work that must be done to keep it clean. The best of the wooden boards are made by electrically (and permanently) bonding strips of wood with synthetic glues.

CUTTING PARTS

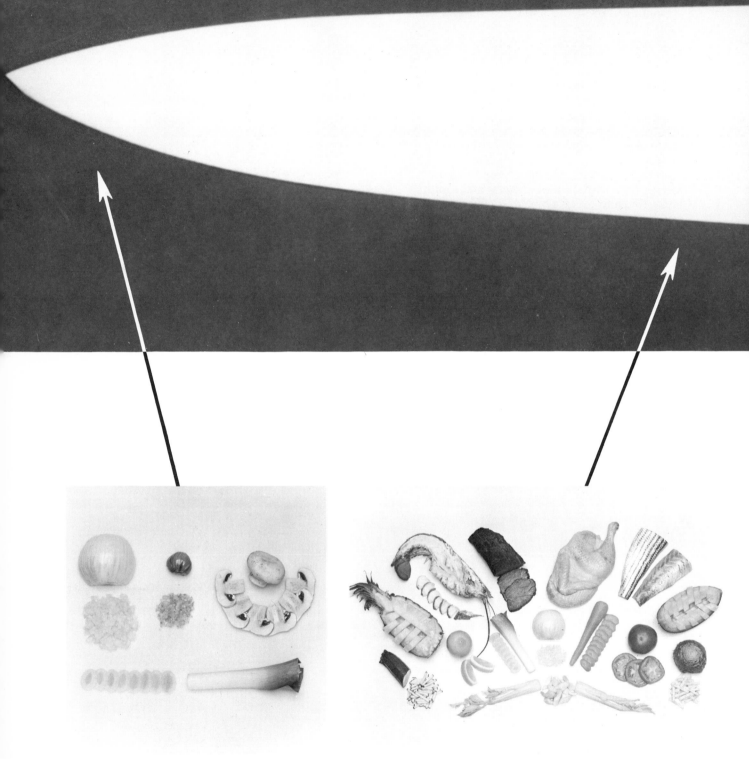

The point and first few inches of the Chef's Knife blade, referred to as the Tip, are the most delicate parts of the tool, and thus are most appropriately used in handling small or delicate items, for example, in slicing mushrooms, slicing shallots, making preliminary cuts in onions and cutting leeks. Never use the point as anything but a tool for cutting food products, as a broken tip seriously diminishes the usefulness of the Chef's Knife.

The most frequently used part of the Chef's Knife is the center of the Cutting Edge. It serves well on firm as well as soft items, with small chops and with long strokes and in attaining end results which are tiny or large.

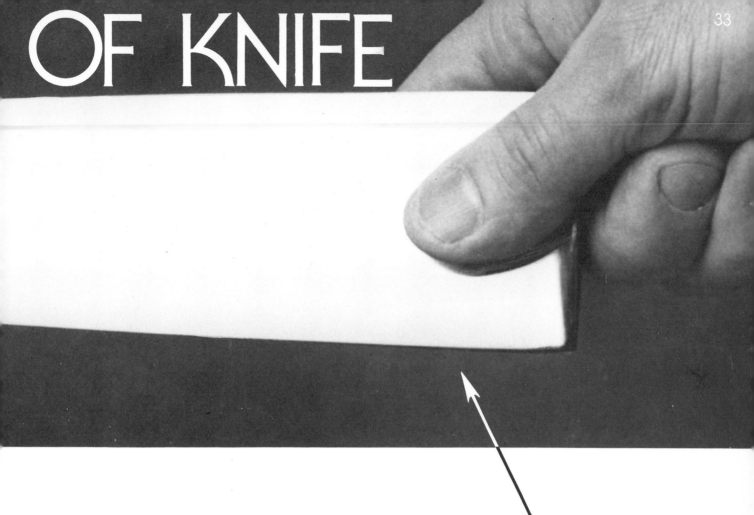

There are no set rules as to what part of the knife must be used to handle specific food items, but the Tip, the center of the Cutting Edge and the Heel are each best suited to certain types of tasks. The rule is to follow the tenets of common sense, to use the Tip for delicate operations, the Heel for the heaviest and the center of the Cutting Edge for the most general and those which require long strokes. Of course, the size of the knife you are using will also influence the area you choose to employ. The type of grip will be influenced by the part of the knife being used, as well as the size of the knife and the size of your hand.

The last few inches of the blade are known as the Heel. It is used mostly for heavy cutting tasks, or when maximum leverage is needed. It is most efficient for making quick, coarse cuts, and for jobs which require strength or pressure.

1. Let the knife rest in your open hand, with your four fingers together at right angles to the knife. The exact place where you grip the knife is a function of how the knife fits comfortably and is kept in control in your hand. The thumb should be relaxed and parallel to the knife.

2. Fold your fingers and, at the same time, tighten the grasp of your palm. The thumb should still be relaxed.

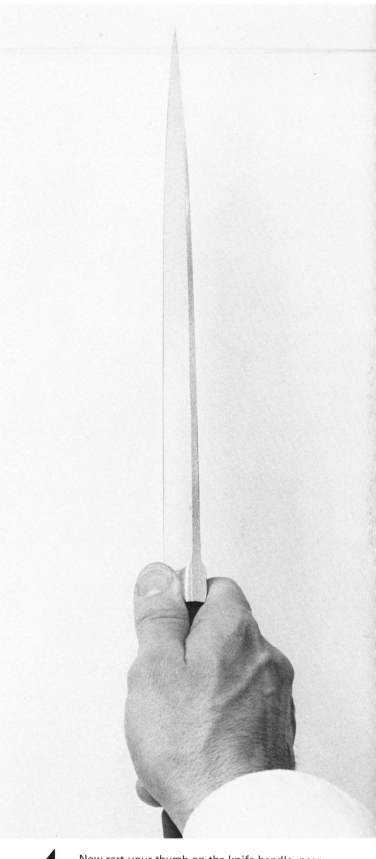

3. Turn the knife so that it is at a right angle to the cutting board and you are ready to begin. Hold the knife securely, not permitting it to rub your hand as you work, which could cause blisters or sore spots.

4. Now rest your thumb on the knife handle, near the index finger. The strength of the grip should still come from the fingers and palm.

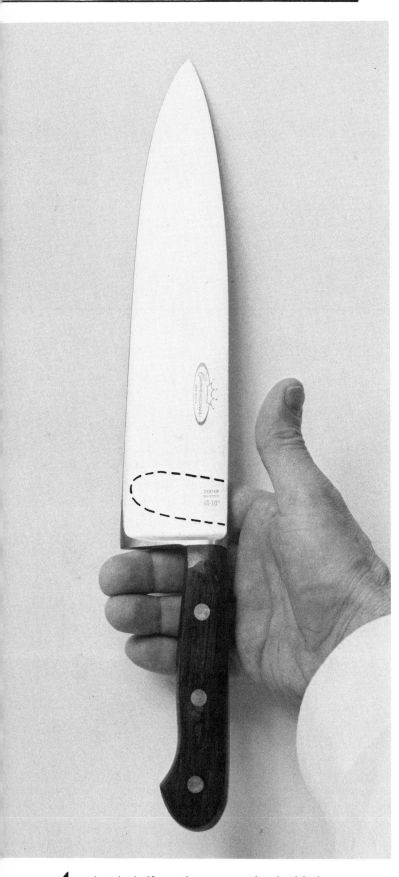

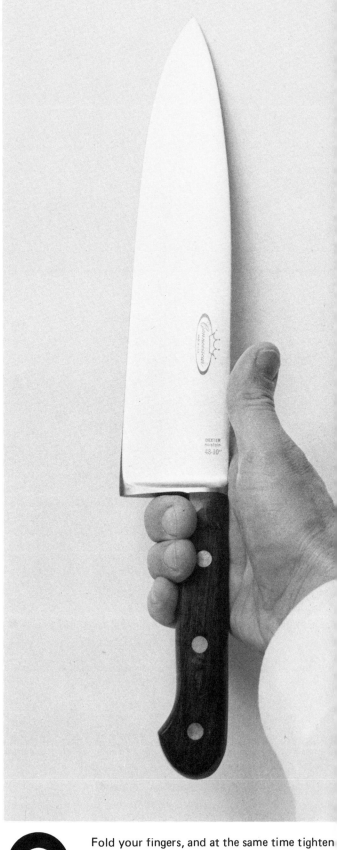

1. Let the knife rest in your open hand, with the index finger on the blade and your other three fingers together, all at right angles to the knife. The exact place where you grip the knife is a function of how the knife fits comfortably and is kept in control in your hand. The thumb should be relaxed and parallel to the knife.

2. Fold your fingers, and at the same time tighten the grasp of your palm. The tip of the index finger should now be touching the bolster and the index finger itself resting flat against the blade. The thumb should still be relaxed.

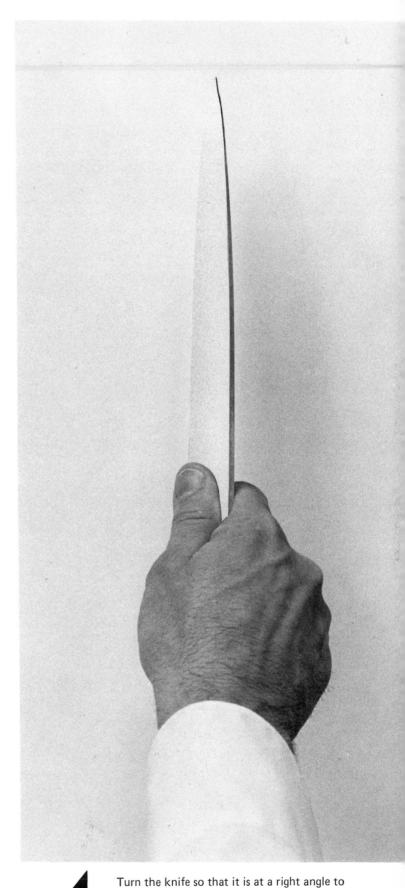

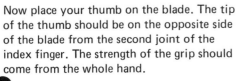 Now place your thumb on the blade. The tip of the thumb should be on the opposite side of the blade from the second joint of the index finger. The strength of the grip should come from the whole hand.

4. Turn the knife so that it is at a right angle to the cutting board and you are ready to begin. Hold the knife securely, not permitting it to rub on your hand as you work, which could cause blisters or sore spots.

1. Let the knife rest in your open hand, the handle lying just before the first finger joints. The exact place where you grip the knife is a function of how the knife fits comfortably and is kept in control in your hand. The thumb should be relaxed and parallel to the knife.

2. Fold your fingers, and at the same time tighten the grasp of your palm. The thumb should still be relaxed.

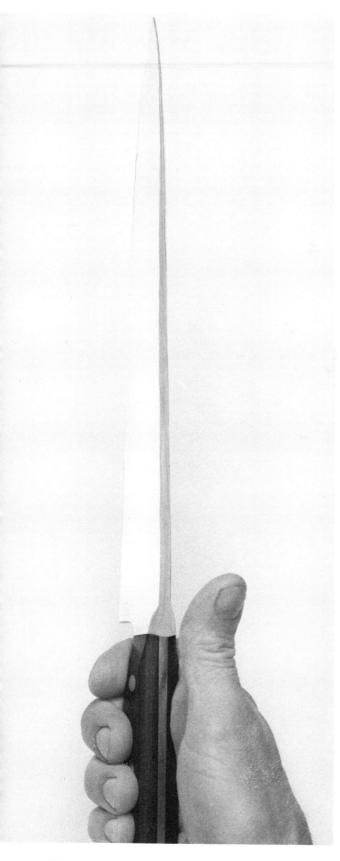

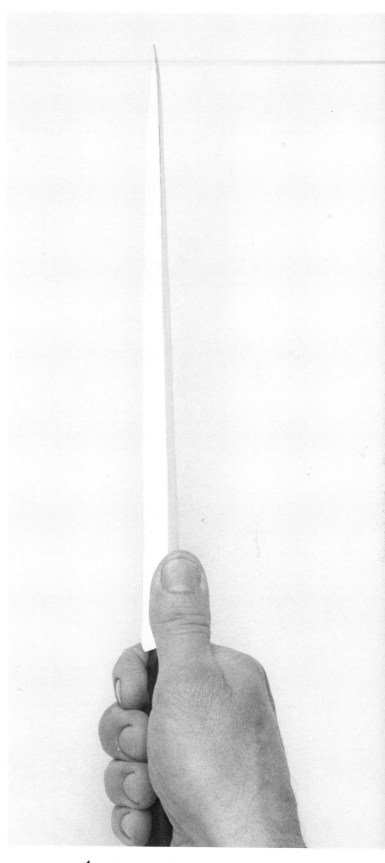

3. Turn the knife so that it is at a right angle to the cutting board.

4. Rest your thumb on the back edge of the blade. The strength of the grip should now come from the whole hand. Hold the knife securely, not permitting it to rub on your hand as you work, which could cause blisters or sore spots.

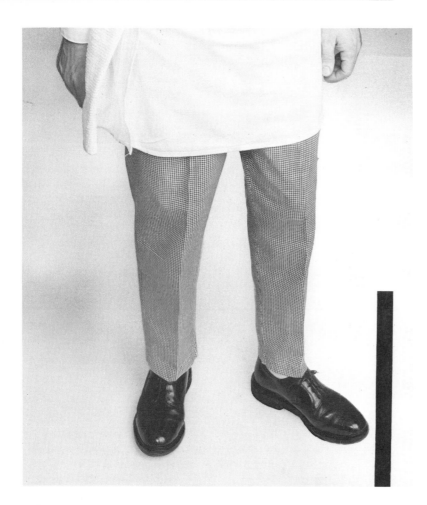

The standing position is an important aspect of handling the Chef's Knife. Not only does a proper standing position make for greater comfort while working, it also increases your efficiency while cutting, and will enable you to work for a longer period of time without becoming fatigued. Either of the standing positions suggested here is acceptable.

Some chefs prefer to stand at an angle to the work table (which they feel gives more freedom of movement) and others work directly in front of the table (which they feel is safer). The standing position you choose is really a function of your preference, what specific item you are cutting and how much space there is in which to move.

1 One foot is slightly behind the other, the front knee is bent, and the body is turned slightly. This stance takes some weight off of the front foot (the left foot for right handed people and right for left handed people).

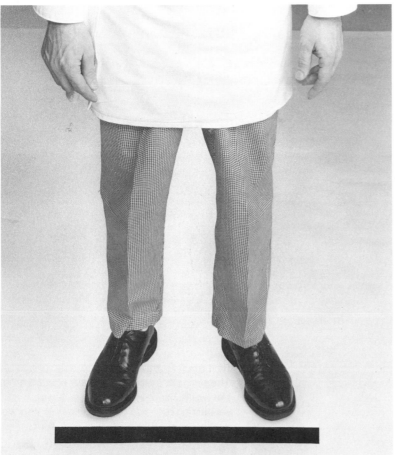

2 The feet are placed evenly and the body is straight. This stance provides even weight distribution between the two feet.

Note: The black line in each picture indicates the position of the work table.

There are three important reasons for taking care in the positioning and movements of the guiding hand, the hand which is not actively holding the Chef's Knife and cutting:

A. *To control slippage* of the item being cut. If we are to work neatly, effectively and safely, it is important that the fruit, vegetable, meat, etc. being cut does not slide on the cutting board. Never try to cut an item with your Chef's Knife unless you have it in control and are certain that it will not slide out from under your knife. This could cause damage to the food product and your hand. Whenever possible, the first cut on a round food item should be to provide a flat base for stability.

B. *To control the size* of the cut. Because the side of the blade touches the fingers on the guiding hand, the hand's position on the item will determine the size cut being made. After each cut, the guiding hand moves back. The distance it moves is determined by how thick you want the next cut to be.

C. *To protect the hand* holding the item being cut. The backs of the fingers rest in contact with the blade and the thumb hidden out of the way. It is virtually impossible for the cutting edge to come into contact with the guiding hand, if proper hand position is used. Bad habits are quick routes to injury. The knife should be at a 90° angle to the cutting board, not facing toward the hand.

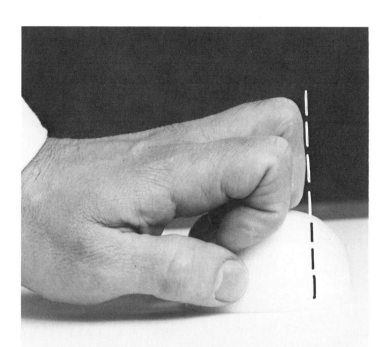

1 This positioning method calls for bent fingers, as the hand actually rests on the item being cut. The thumb and little finger should be parallel to each other and the three other fingers fairly close together. *Note how the blade should rest against the knuckle, which provides guidance but is in no danger of being cut.*

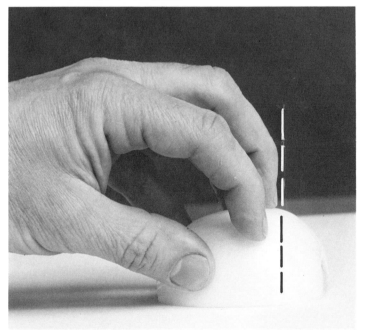

2 This positioning method places the thumb and little finger parallel to each other on the item being cut, the middle finger at the summit, and the other two fingers evenly spaced between them. This is a very firm, effective grip. *Note the way in which the fingers are bent; the blade will rest against the knuckle, providing guidance, but in no danger of cutting the hand.*

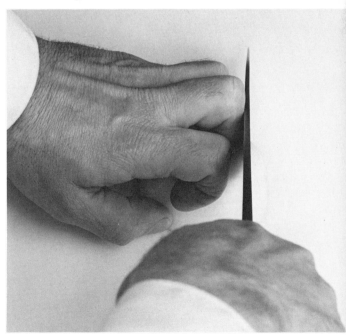

3 The most important aspect to note in this picture is the contact between the knife and the guiding hand, which is not in any danger of being cut by the blade.

NOTE: When cutting extremely small items the fingers may be held vertical, or the index finger alone might serve as the guiding hand.

The Chef's Knife is a versatile tool, not because it is complicated, but because of the many ways in which a skilled hand can work it. In order to develop this accomplished hand, it is important to study, analyze, and practice the many cutting techniques used in handling your knife.

The examples shown in this section are illustrative of some of the most important motions of the Chef's Knife. These all can be easily mastered through practice and through developing coordination, continuity and a smooth, rolling motion in handling the knife. This rhythm will take a great deal of concentration at first, but with practice, the smooth motion of a professional handling his/her knife will come almost naturally to you. The technique used to cut a specific item is determined by the type of knife and the item being cut.

Only in the chopping motion (No. 2) does the product move on the cutting board. For the best results, the guiding hand and the knife move, not the food item.

Motion No. 1 - The Heel End as the Cutting Edge

1 The blade is placed on the item to be cut. Note that the tip is pointing slightly upward.

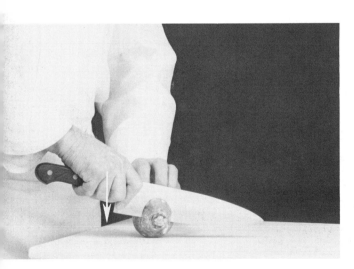

2 The cut begins with a downward motion which also moves the knife into a more horizontal position.

3 The cut ends as the blade reaches the cutting board. Note the area of the blade which has been used and that horizontal as well as vertical movement has been used.

Motion No. 2 - Chopping - for parsley and similar fine tasks which do not require a precisely shaped product.

1 This continuous, fast motion begins with the knife held high and the guiding hand gently providing just enough pressure to hold it in control and always in contact with the cutting board.

2 Lower the knife, looking ahead to anticipate where you want to cut.

3 Continue, beginning to cut, as the curved edge of the blade comes into contact with the board.

4 The heel of the knife is now in contact with the board and every inch of the blade has been utilized in the cutting action.

Raise the knife to its original position, preparing to perform exactly the same operation, this time coming down in a different place very close to the original cut. Repeat Steps No. 1-4, redistributing the product on the cutting board if necessary, until the food is as finely chopped as necessary.

Motion No. 3 - The Main Cutting Edge

1 Hold the knife at about a 45 degree angle to the cutting board, touching the object being cut (which is being held securely by the guiding hand).

2 The cutting action is in bringing the knife forward and downward while letting it become more horizontal.

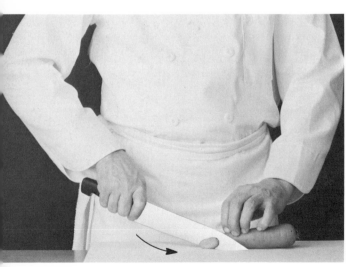

3 The cut continues in a smooth motion. Note how the blade is continually in contact with the cutting board.

4 The cut ends as the blade, now horizontal, reaches the cutting board. To make the second cut using this technique, lift the knife to its position in Step No. 1, keeping it constantly in contact with the cutting board. During the upward motion, move the guiding hand to determine the size of the next cut.

Motion No. 4 - The Tip and Center as a Cutting Edge - Large Object

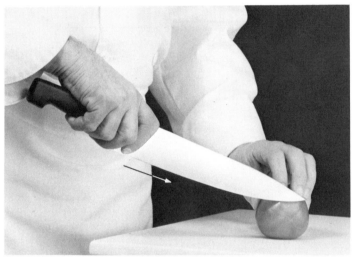

1 Hold the knife touching the top of the object being cut (which is being held securely by the guiding hand). The size of the angle will be a function of the size of the object you are cutting.

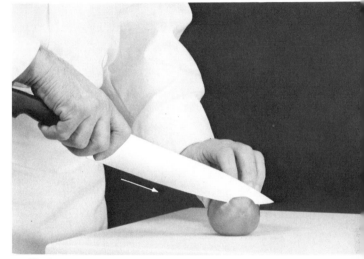

2 The cutting action is in bringing the knife forward and downward.

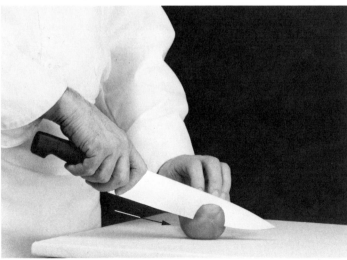

3 The cut continues in a smooth motion. Note that the angle of the knife has not changed significantly.

4 As soon as the knife has contact with the cutting board, bring it to a horizontal position. To make the second cut utilizing this technique, lift the knife to its position in Step No. 1 while moving the guiding hand to determine the size of the next cut.

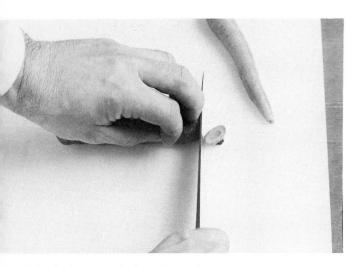

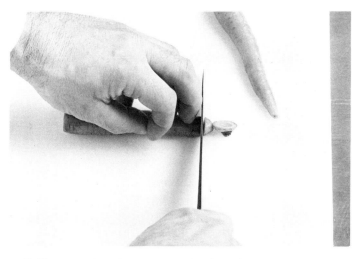

1 Wash the carrot before placing it on your clean cutting board. The first cut is to remove the stem end, wasting as little as possible. You may be able to utilize this piece in the stock pot.

2 The second cut is to remove the tip end, wasting as little as possible. This may also be used in the stock pot.

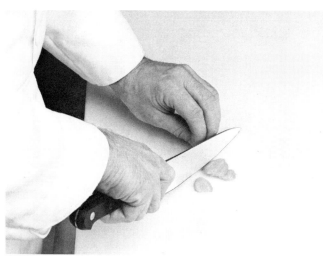

3 Start the smooth motion of the cut with the knife in a 45° angle position.

4 Continue the movement, cutting through the carrot as the knife is constantly in contact with the cutting board.

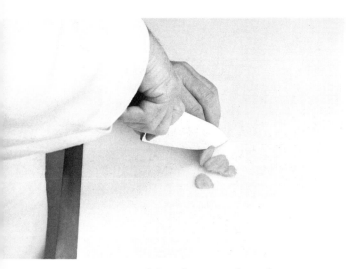

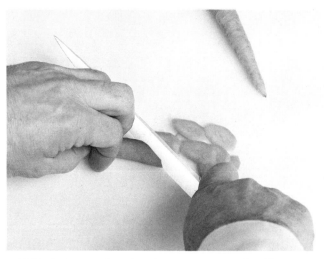

5 Complete the cut, and then, in a smooth motion, move the knife back to the 45° angle position. The smooth motion and careful guiding hand will be rewarded with a series of even cuts.

6 Variation: performing the cuts on an angle will result in oval rather than circular slices.

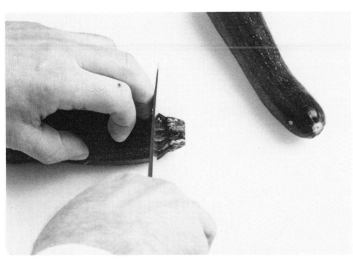

1 Wash the squash (and, if necessary, peel lightly) before placing it on your clean cutting board. The first cut is to remove the stem end, wasting as little as possible.

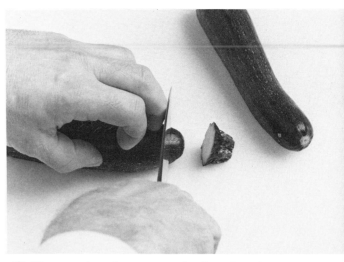

2 The second cut is to remove the tip end, again wasting as little as possible.

3 Make cuts across the length of the zucchini. The size of the cuts will be determined by the size of the squash and the size dice you desire.

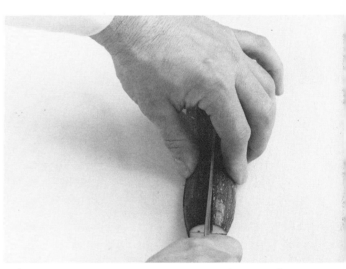

4 Turn the squash so that cuts made in Step No. 3 are parallel to the cutting board. Make at least one cut across the length of the zucchini.

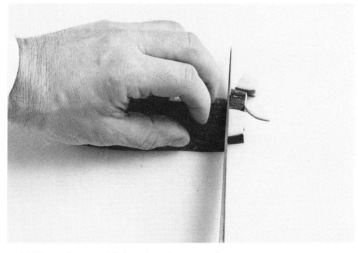

5 Turn the zucchini and make even slices across the width.

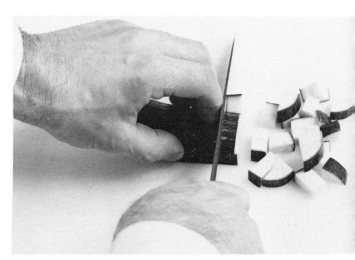

6 The pieces of zucchini will be of similar size.

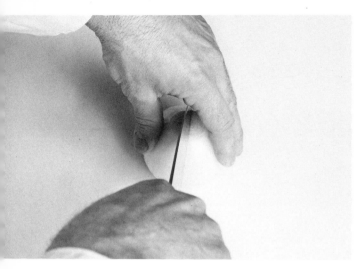

1 Place the peeled onion, root side down, on the cutting board.

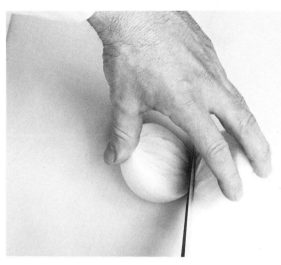

2 Cut the onion lengthwise, cutting toward the root end. Follow the natural stripes.

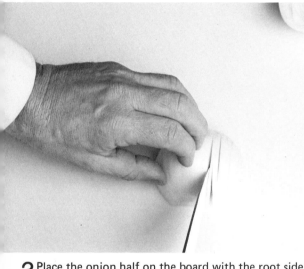

3 Place the onion half on the board with the root side away from you. Make lengthwise cuts, being careful not to cut through the root (which will help hold the onion together).

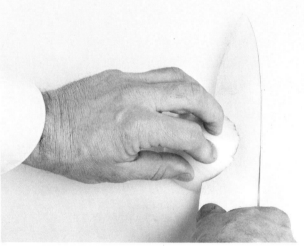

4 Hold the partially shredded onion together with the guiding hand. Make a cut toward the root end at an angle. Be careful not to cut all the way through the onion.

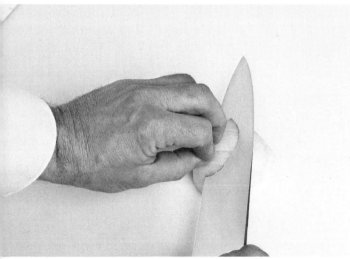

5 Make a second cut, also on an angle, somewhat higher. Depending on the size of the onion, you may need to make one or two more of these cuts. Always be careful to hold the onion together and to keep from cutting all the way through.

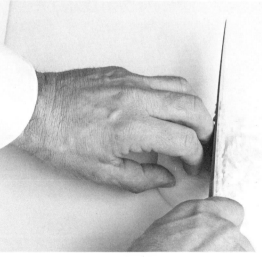

6 Make slices across the grain of the onion, being careful to hold the onion intact with the guiding hands. As shown in the picture, the onion will be diced. The dice size will be a function of the cut size, and of the size of the onion.

1 Peel the potato and remove eyes and any imperfections.

2 Make a total of six cuts around the potato to make it into a box shape. Reserve the parings for mashed potatoes, soups, or other uses.

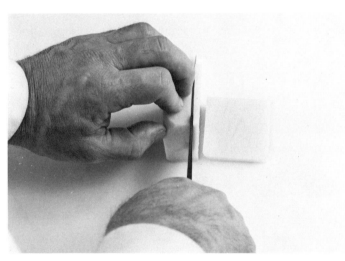

3 Make your first slice into the potato, being careful that it is the proper size.

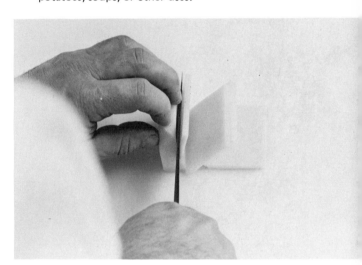

4 Subsequent slices should be of the same size as the first, and the resulting potato squares should be nearly identical.

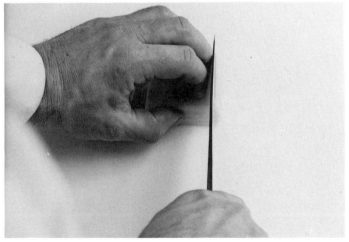

5 Rebuild the potato, with the squares stacked on top of each other. Hold the potato carefully, and make your first cut exactly the same width as the slices in Steps No. 3 and No. 4.

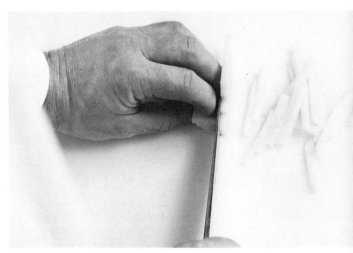

6 The result will be evenly sized batonnets of potato. Variation: To dice potatoes, make another cut of the same size across the batonnets; the result will be perfect cubes.

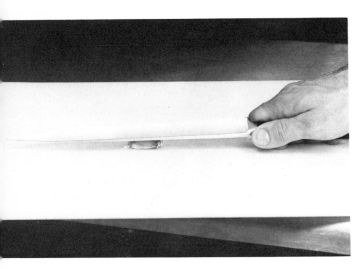

1 Place the garlic clove on your clean cutting board, and lay the Chef's Knife atop it.

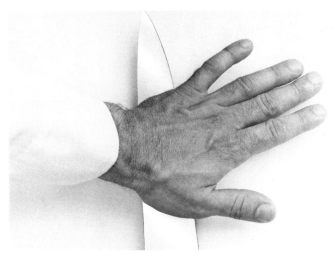

2 With a single, firm stroke, apply pressure to the top of the knife. This will loosen the outer skin of the garlic clove.

3 Peel the garlic clove. Remove the brown spot on the root end as well as any blemishes on the garlic.

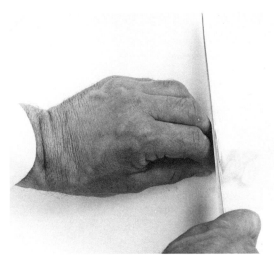

4 Make very thin slices in the garlic clove. Chop coarsely, using the motion shown on page 43.

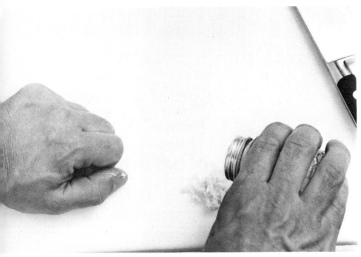

5 OPTIONAL STEP
Sprinkle the chopped garlic with salt. The salt will help to provide abrasion which facilitates crushing. Also, the salt absorbs oils which might otherwise be absorbed into the cutting board.

6 The crushing is accomplished by the knife actually smearing the garlic on the board. Place the knife atop the garlic so that the blade is almost horizontal. Pushing down on the knife, press it across the garlic. Do not push toward the blade.

One of the most common uses of the Chef's Knife is in preparing mirepoix, the coarsely cut vegetables named for the Duke of Mirepoix, an eighteenth century Frenchman. An important thing to remember about mirepoix cuts is that the product need not be absolutely precise; it is going to cook for a long time to release its flavor in the roasting pan or stock pot and be discarded or, perhaps, pureed.

Cutting mirepoix is a good way to practice using your Chef's Knife. You might even want to practice some of the more complex cuts on carrots, celery and onions, then use the items as mirepoix.

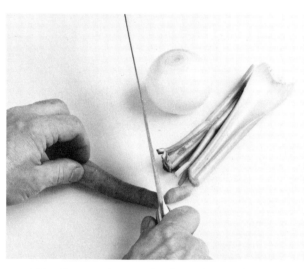

1 The first step is to peel, trim and clean the vegetables. Certain trimmings may be used in the stock pot.

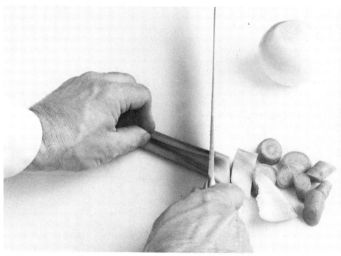

2 Cut the carrot coarsely, in chunks about 1 inch (2.54 cm) in length. Celery is cut coarsely, also in 1 inch chunks.

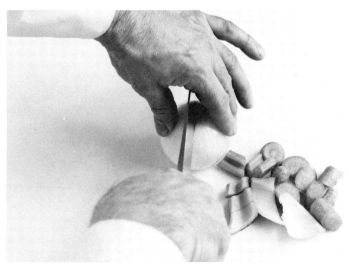

3 Cut the onion in half lengthwise (through the root end). Then use the same technique as for Dicing Onions (page 48) to cut very large (1 inch) chunks.

4 The resulting vegetables will be of similar size.

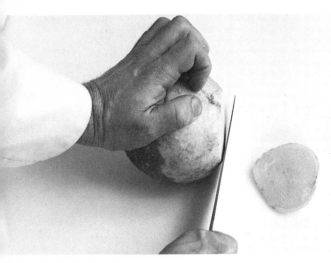

1 Wash the rutabaga (or Swedish turnip) before placing it on its side on your clean cutting board. Cut off the small bump on the bottom.

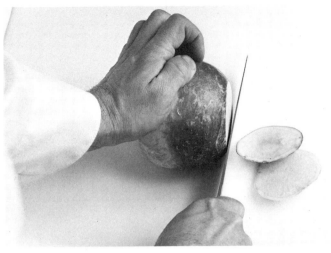

2 Turn the rutabaga around. Cut off the stem end.

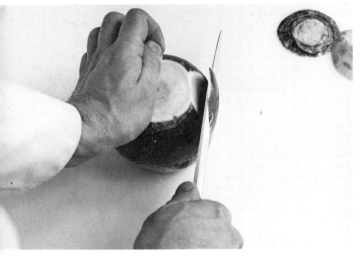

3 Place the rutabaga on the board with the flat, bottom side down. Start removing the heavy skin by making a narrow vertical slice, following the contours of the vegetable.

4 Continue the same procedure all around the rutabaga, turning it slightly before each cut. Cut deep enough to remove the second (bitter) skin, but do not try to economize on the number of cuts you make by making the cuts too deep (which is wasteful).

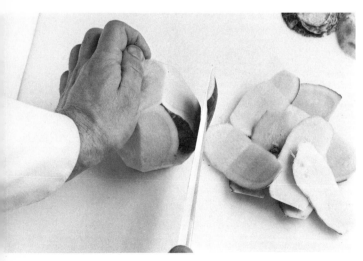

5 Try to make the cuts even, as shown in the picture.

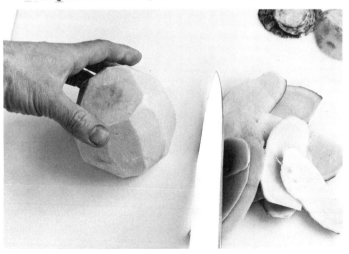

6 The finished product will be free of skin, and with even sides all around.

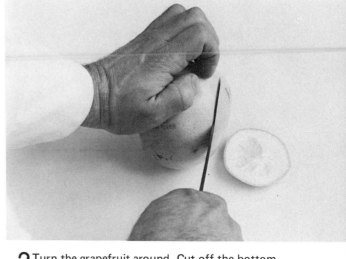

1 Place the grapefruit on its side. Use a stainless steel knife to cut off the top, slicing only deeply enough to remove the rind and white pith.

2 Turn the grapefruit around. Cut off the bottom, slicing only deeply enough to remove the rind and white pith.

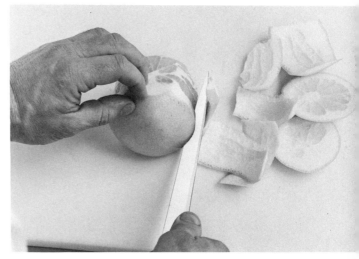

3 Set the grapefruit on a flat side for stability. Make the first vertical cut, slicing only deeply enough to remove the rind and white pith and a very small amount of fruit.

4 Continue the procedure around the grapefruit, turning it slightly before each cut. Do not try to economize on the number of cuts you make by making the cuts too deep (which is wasteful).

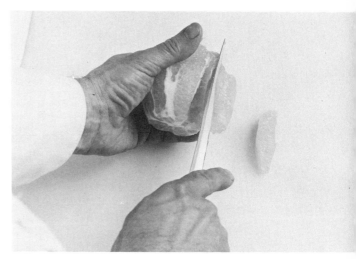

5 By the time the cuts are finished, the grapefruit should be nearly 100% free of rind and pith.

6 To make sections, hold the grapefruit firmly in your hand. Look for the natural separations, and gently free the sections with the tip of your knife; this should not require a great deal of pressure.

1 Place the pineapple on the cutting board, the leafy end toward you. Place the stainless steel knife on the pineapple, at the far end, and begin to cut the fruit in half, with a firm, smooth stroke. The knife will start at a nearly 90° angle and gradually be lowered.

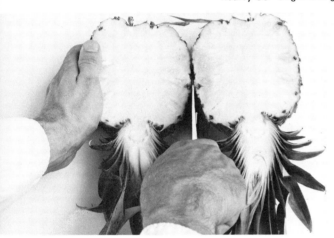

2 As the cut is finished, the knife will approach a horizontal position. The pineapple will be in nearly perfect halves.

3 Using a similar stroke, cut each of the pieces in half.

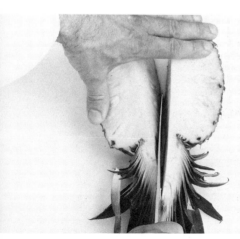

4 Again, the knife started in a nearly vertical position and finished in a nearly horizontal position.

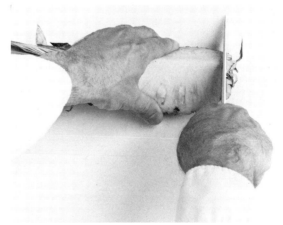

5 Grasp the pineapple quarter firmly. With a single, firm stroke, cut off the tip.

6 Hold the pineapple in a vertical position, which will be stable because of the flat surface created by cutting off the tip. Begin to slice off the fibrous center core. Complete the cut in a smooth fashion.

7 Stand the pineapple on the cutting board. Hold firmly and carefully begin to cut the fruit from the rind, cutting with a downward motion. (It is advisable to check the underside of the fruit for 'eyes' of rind, which may be removed with the tip of the Chef's Knife.)

8 Holding the fruit in place on the rind, cut in half lengthwise.

9 Makes a series of cuts about 3/4 inch (1.9 cm) apart to create chunks.

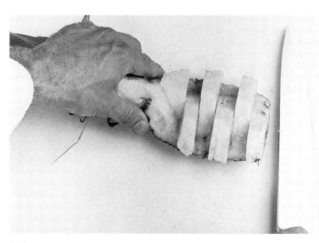

10 Variation: Omitting Step No. 8 and arranging the pineapple chunks as shown in the photograph above makes for an attractive presentation.

BASIC LEEK PREPARATION

The basic steps on this page may be followed by
more cuts to mince or slice the leeks. Leeks
harvested during the month of July often have
a woody core which should be removed
after halving.

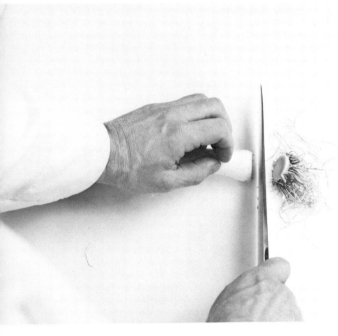

1 Rinse off the leek before placing it on your clean cutting
board. Remove the root, cutting off as little as possible,
with one stroke of the Chef's Knife.

2 Hold the root end up, with the green leafy end resting
on the cutting board. Trim the ends.

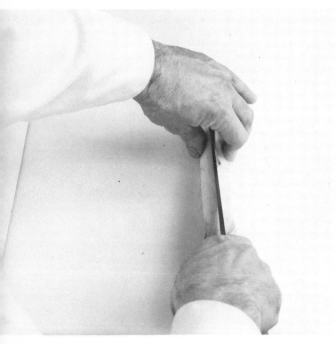

3 Hold the leek flat on the cutting board. Place the knife
on top, and make a cut through the root end.

4 Continue through the length of the leek until it is in
two halves.

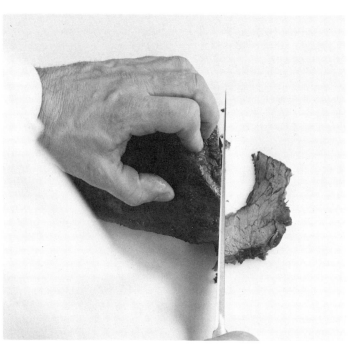

1 Place the meat on the cutting board, so that it rests securely. With a smooth movement of the Chef's Knife,* make the first slice. Cut across the grain.

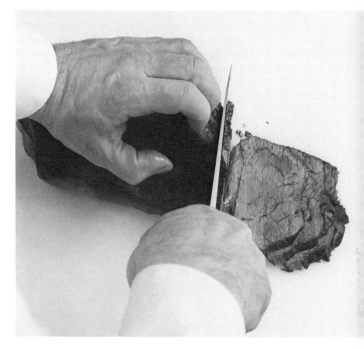

2 Continue to cut, moving the guiding hand across the meat and making smooth, even slices in long sweeps, using the full cutting edge. The knife should be somewhat vertical at the beginning of the cuts; you should maintain eye contact with the back of the knife.

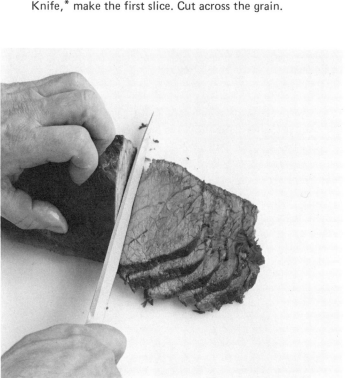

3 The knife becomes more horizontal as it glides through the meat.

NOTE: *A special meat slicing knife, if available, is the best tool for this task.

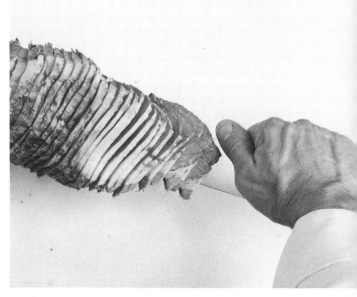

4 To pick up the cooked meat, gently slide the Chef's Knife under the slices. The guiding hand holds the meat as it is lifted and moved onto a plate. Should the meat start to slide off of the knife, do not attempt to catch it, as your hand could be cut.

1 Place the chicken (or other type of bird) on the cutting board, breast down, and with the wings closest to you. Grasp the tail and make an incision to the right of it (left-handed individuals should make this cut on the left of the tail).

2 Continue cutting, immediately to the right of the back.

3 Finish the cut by completely opening the back of the chicken, always cutting immediately to the right of the backbone.

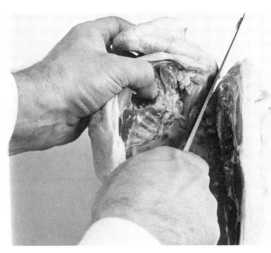

4 Turn the chicken so that the tail end is closest to you. The next step is to release the breastbone. Make a cut to break the wishbone, which will loosen the bone structure of the bird.

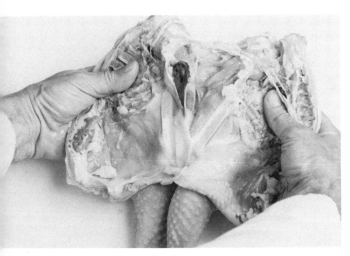

5 Pull the chicken open utilizing enough force to separate the flesh from the cartilage and breastbone.

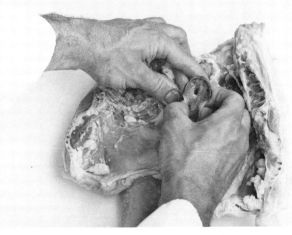

6 Grasp the breastbone and pull it toward you; the cartilage attached to it should be removed in this same movement.

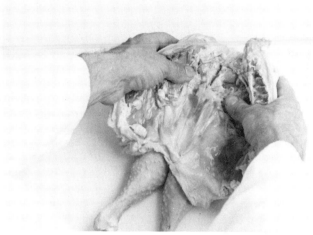

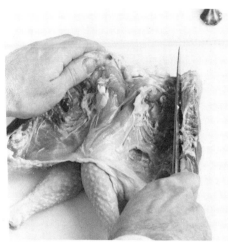

7 The next step is to further loosen the bone structure. Grasp the thigh in one hand and the section of the chicken to which it is attached in the other. Bend the chicken back until the joint of the thigh and the breast is popped. Repeat on the other side.

8 The next step is to remove the backbone. Place the knife adjacent to the backbone, as close as possible.

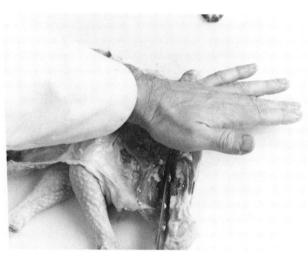

9 With a single motion of the length of the knife, cut through the chicken to release the entire backbone.

10 The next step is to remove the cartilage at the end of the legs. Place the knive on the very tip of the leg, exactly where you intend to cut.

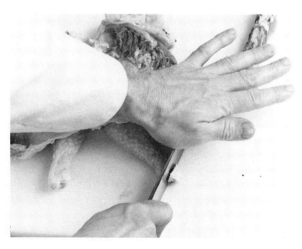

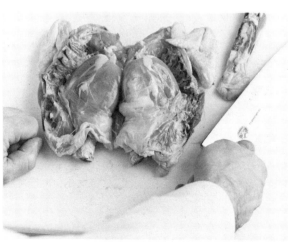

11 Lower the hand not holding the knife to drive the edge through the cartilage. Be careful not to splinter the leg bone.

12 The split chicken may be left whole, or may be cut in half between the two meaty portions of the breast.

SPLITTING LOBSTER

1 Place the lobster on the cutting board facing away from you. With a firm, deliberate movement of the knife, cut off the legs on the right side of the lobster.

2 Turn the lobster around, so that it is facing you. With a firm, deliberate stroke, cut off the legs on the lobster's left side.

3 With the tip of the knife, make a cut in the head, cutting through the shell. Remove the sand bag, which is inedible.

4 Turn the lobster around, so that it is facing away from you. Place the Chef's Knife on the lobster lined up with the head cut, and with a firm push, cut the lobster in half. Remove the nerve strip.

5 Grasp the claw firmly in your hand and position your Chef's Knife above it, *the blade side up.*

6 With a swift motion, crack the claw *with the back side of the knife.*

NOTE: The lobster in these photographs is cooked. If you are dealing with a live lobster, it would be more humane to follow Steps No. 3 and No. 4 first, to kill the lobster, then go back to No. 1 and No. 2.

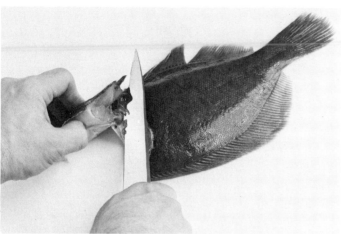

1 The first step in fileting a (raw) flat fish is to remove the head. Place the Chef's Knife, preferably a small, flexible model*, under the gills and begin to exert pressure to start the cut. Continue the cut, releasing the head, which should be gently pulled away from the body of the fish.

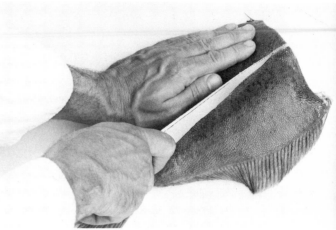

2 Place the fish on the cutting board with the tail end toward you. Make a shallow cut along the backbone.

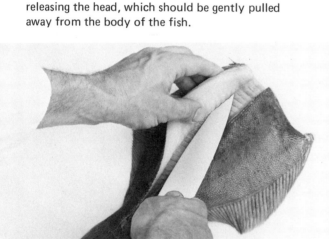

3 Make a series of long, smooth cuts, parallel to the backbone, to gently separate the flesh of the fish from the bone.

4 When the last of these long, smooth cuts is made, the filet will be released from the bone, and should be in one piece.

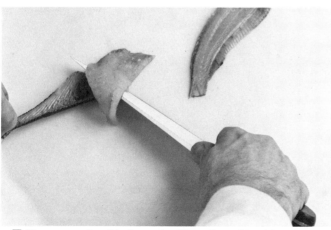

5 To remove the skin from the filet, place skin-side down on the cutting board (at the edge of the bench or table), the narrow end toward you.

NOTE: *A special fish fileting knife (if available) is the best tool for this task.

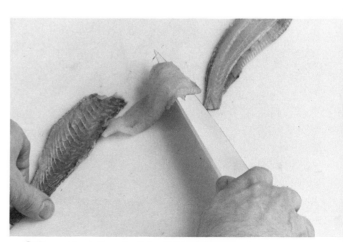

6 Grasp the tail end of the fish, placing the tip of the knife (as parallel as possible to the board) on the filet adjacent to the tail. Scrape the skin, thus releasing the flesh of the fish, while pulling on the tail.

The photographs on these two pages illustrate the relative sizes of many classical types of cuts. Potatoes (*pommes*, in French) were used for all of the examples.

**POMMES PAILLES/JULIENNE
STRAW OR SHOESTRING POTATOES
2 in. x 1/16 in. x 1/16 in.
5 cm x 1.6 mm x 1.6 mm**

**FINE BRUNOISE
1/16 in. x 1/16 in. x 1/16 in.
1.6 mm x 1.6 mm x 1.6 mm**

**POMMES ALLUMETTES
MATCHSTICK POTATOES
2 1/2 in. x 1/8 in. x 1/8 in.
6.4 cm x 3.2 mm x 3.2 mm**

**REGULAR BRUNOISE
1/8 in. x 1/8 in. x 1/8 in.
3.2 mm x 3.2 mm x 3.2 mm**

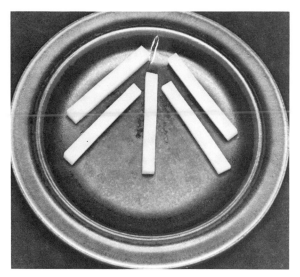

POMMES BATONNETTES
LONG BRANCH/BATONNET POTATOES
2 1/2 in. x 1/4 in. x 1/4 in.
6.4 cm x 6.4 mm x 6.4 mm

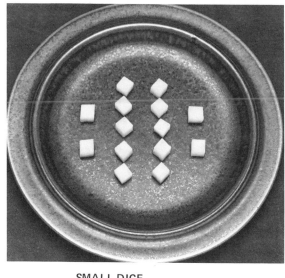

SMALL DICE
1/4 in. x 1/4 in. x 1/4 in.
6.4 mm x 6.4 mm x 6.4 mm

POMMES FRITES
STANDARD FRENCH FRIES
2 1/2 in. x 1/3 in. x 1/3 in.
6.4 cm x 8.5 mm x 8.5 mm

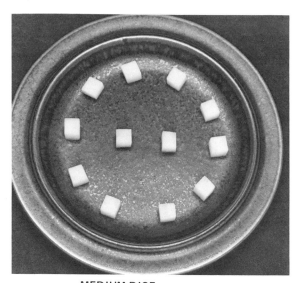

MEDIUM DICE
1/3 in. x 1/3 in. x 1/3 in.
8.5 mm x 8.5 mm x 8.5 mm

POMMES PONT NEUF
LARGE FRENCH FRIES
3 in. x 3/4 in. x 3/4 in.
7.6 cm x 2 cm x 2 cm

LARGE DICE
3/4 in. x 3/4 in. x 3/4 in.
2 cm x 2 cm x 2 cm

INDEX

The following firms contributed products and/or advice for this text:

J & D Brauner, Inc. - *Cutting Board*
R. H. Forschner Co., Inc. (Forschner, Dick, Victorinox) -
    Knives and Sharpening Steels
Russell Harrington Cutlery, Inc. (Dexter) -
    Knives and Sharpeining Steels
J. A. Henkels - *Knives and Sharpening Steels*
Northeast Restaurant Supply, Inc. - *Cutting Board*
Norton-Abrasive Sales Co. - *Sharpening Stones*
Park Rubber Co. - *Cutting Board*
Poli Brothers (Sabatier) - *Storage Rack and Knives*
Rowoco (Sabatier) - *Knives, Sharpening Steel, Storage Rack*
Alfred Zanger Co. - *Cutting Board, Sharpening Steel, Storage Rack*